ITALIAN

by
Susanne Weller

Hayit Publishing

ITALIA

MARE MEDITE

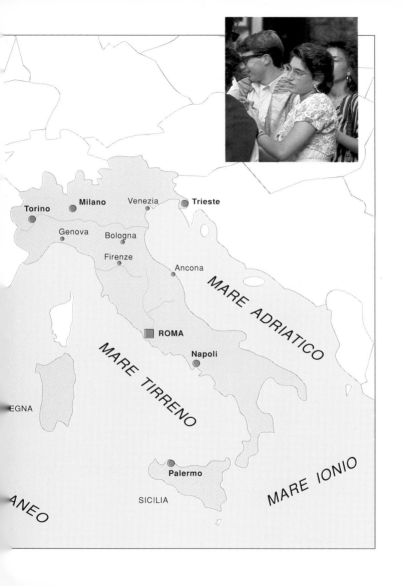

Torino

Milano   Venezia   Trieste

Genova   Bologna

Firenze

Ancona

MARE ADRIATICO

ROMA

Napoli

MARE TIRRENO

EGNA

ANEO

Palermo

SICILIA

MARE IONIO

1st Edition 1994
ISBN 1-874251-18-5

© copyright 1994
   Hayit Publishing GB, Ltd, London/England

© copyright 1994 original version
   Hayit Verlag GmbH, Cologne/Germany

Author: Susanne Weller
Editor: Petra Juling
Translation, Adaption, Revision: Scott Reznik
Assistant Editor (English version): Sabarah Hanif
Print: Sutter & Partner, Essen/Germany
Map: Ulrich Berger-Juling Electronic Publishing, Bonn/Germany
Typesetting: Anglia Marketing, Cologne/Germany
Title Photo: Transglobe
Photos: ENIT, Düsseldorf; Hayit Verlag Archives; Astrid Leibisch; Christoph
Schmutte; Cay Rademacher; Susanne Weller
Illustrations: Reinald Gerhards, Veronika Richter

Preface

Those travelling in a foreign country where the language is just as foreign will encounter some difficult situations in making themselves understood. This language guide is conceived to help international travellers in a number of situations.

The first section of this book includes remarks on pronunciation as well as a brief summary of the most important aspects of Italian grammar. In the sections to follow, the focus is not on liguistic precision, but on the use of the language in the simplest way possible. For this reason, pronunciations must be viewed as approximations since many foreign languages contain sounds which are virtually unknown in the English language.

Only the most important phases and imparative aspects of the language necessary for travel are covered in this book.

The actual phrase section is subdivided into ten thematic chapters: the most important phrases as a basis – whether it be linguistic etiquette or numbers, days of the week, months, the time or the weather – are listed first.

Following this are phrases and vocabulary lists relating to nine specific situations which the traveller will encounter: from travelling by train, plane and car; from accommodation and restaurants; all the way to (hopefully unnecessary) a visit to the doctor. The beginning of each chapter covers simple phrases for the given situation followed by alphabetical vocabulary lists intended to help the reader quickly pinpoint the correct word.

Each page is made up of three columns: to the left is the English term or phrase, to the right of this is the Italian word or phrase. The third column contains the pronunciation using a simplified phoenetic alphabet. The exception to this rule: restaurant menus. This is because these are primarily in the foreign language. With the help of our simplified phoenetic entries, the pronunciation of the language is rendered in the easiest way possible. With some languages, however, phoeneitc symbols cannot be avoided.

In order to facilitate the quick location of an appropriate word without having to page through the entire book, we include an extensive glossary at the back of the book: all important terms used in the phrase sections are repeated with the translation, listed alphabetically. First from English to Italian and then from Italian to English.

We hope that Hayit's Phrase Books are a practical help wherever your travels may take you. We wish you the best on your trip and a pleasant stay.

Hayit Publishing

CONTENTS

Introduction

Phoenetics
The phonetic alphabet used in this phrase book is *not* that normally used in foreign language dictionaries, the International Phonetic Alphabet. This book implements letters and combinations to closely approximate the pronunciation as one would normally pronounce them in English. For this reason, no advance knowledge of, or experience in speaking the language is necessary. The following is an explanation of the pronunciations of letters and combinations. The fact that these are only approximations of sounds and colourations is unavoidable and we hope that linguists and those with advanced knowledge and skills in the Italian language will accept these as such.

Italian Pronunciation at a Glance

Vowels
The e in an Italian word is pronounced like a long a as the *eh* sound in "day" or as a a short e as in the word "set".
The o is either pronounced long as *oh* as in "zone" or it is a short *ò* as in the word "hot".
The a can also be long or short: *ah* as in "hall" or a somewhat shorter *à* as in "what".
The i in Italian takes on the *ee* sound as in "see".
The u can be long and short, like the *uh* sound in "shoe" or sort like the *ù* sound in "book".
There are no dipthongs, meaning that each vowel retains its sound; thus, the word Europa is not pronounced *yuhroh'pah* but *eh'urohpah*

Consonants
Most consonants are pronounced as they are in English with the following exceptions:

letter	phoenetic symbol	pronunciation
c	*ch*	pronounced like a *ch* as in "cherry" if it precedes the vowels e and i, for example centro *(chentroh)* or circolo *(cheerkoloh)*
	k	before the vowels a, o, and u as well as preceeding an h, the c is pronounced as a k as in cantina *(kahnteenah)* , Colonia

		(Kohlohneeah), curva *(kuhrvah),* chiamare *(kjahmahreh)*
g	*j*	when preceeding an e or i, the g is pronounced as a *j* like the soft g in "gentlemen", for example gente *(jenteh),* ginnastica *(jinahsteekah)*
	g	when followed by an a, o, u or h, the g is pronounced like the hard g in "gate", for example galante *(gahlanteh),* golfo *(golfoh),* gusto *(gùstoh),* paghiamo *(pahgyahmoh)*
gl	*ly*	for example voglia *(vohlyah)*
gn	*ny*	for example bisogno *(beezònyoh)*
r	*r*	the r should be rolled on the tounge
s	*s*	the s is usually pronounced as a hard *s,*
	z	however, it is pronounced as a *z* before the consonants b, d, g, l, m, n, r or v. Examples: strada *(strahdah)* – sdraia *(zdrahyah),* turismo *(tureezmoh)*

Accenting Syllables

The main accent on Italian words is usually on the second to last syllable, for example buono, leggero, ragazzo, parlare.

A series of words have the main accent on the third to last syllable, for instance giovane, facile, tavola, telefono, Genova.

Several words have the accent on the last syllable. The emphasis is then indicated by an accent sign: città, gioventù, caffè, più, perchè. In cases where the emphasis is not obvious, the emphasis is indicated by a bar below the appropriate syllable in the phonetic entries.

The Alphabet and Spelling

A *(ah)*	**I** *(ee)*	**S** *(eseh)*
B *(bee)*	**L** *(eleh)*	**T** *(tee)*
C *(chee)*	**M** *(emeh)*	**U** *(ùh)*
D *(dee)*	**N** *(eneh)*	**V** *(vee)*
E *(eh)*	**O** *(ò)*	**W** *(dòpyah vee)*
F *(efeh)*	**P** *(pee)*	**X** *(iks)*
G *(djee)*	**Q** *(kuh)*	**Y** *(ipseelòn)*
H *(ahkah)*	**R** *(ehreh)*	**Z** *(dzehtah)*

A Brief Introduction to Grammar

Types of Words
The Articles
In the Italian Language, there are masculine and feminine words, but no neuter.

The masculine definite article is *il* in the singular and *i* in the plural form. Example: *il libro* (the book), *i libri (the books)*.

The feminie definite article is *la* in the singular and *le in* the plural form. Example: *la pagina* (the page), *le pagine (the pages)*.

One exception to this rule can be found with masculine words beginning with a z or an s followed by a consonant, meaning sb, sc, sd, sp etc. Then the definite article is *lo* instead of *il* in the singular and *gli* instead of *i* in the plural. Examples: *lo zaino* (the backpack), *gli zaini* (the backpacks), *lo specchio* (the mirror), *gli specchi* (the mirrors).

•   Masculine words beginning with a vowel (a, e, i, o or u) also take on the article *lo* in the singlular and *gli* in the plural. Example: *l'anno* (the year), *gli anni* (the years).

•   When preceding a vowel (a, e, i, o and u), both the masculine *lo* and the feminine *la* are shortened to *l'* in the singular; thus, *l'alvero* (the tree), *l'amica* (the girlfriend).

The definite article, unlike other languages, appears in front of possessive pronouns: *la mia chave* (my key), *le nostre amiche* (our girlfriends). One important aspect to note is that members of one's family and close relatives do not have a definite article in the singular; thus: *mia sorella* (my sister), *tua madre* (your mother), *nostro zio* (our uncle) etc.

The indefinite article (a, an) is *un* for masculine words, *una* for feminine words and *uno* for those words that have *lo* as their definite article. Examples: *un, libro, una pagina, uno specchio*.

When preceding a vowel, *uno* is shortened to *un* and *una* to *un'*. Examples: *un anno, un'amica*.

Nouns
■   Gender
Almost all nouns ending in *-o* are masculine; those ending in *-a*, feminine: *il ragazzo* (the boy), *la sera* (the evening). Nouns ending in *-e* can be masculine or feminine: *il latte* (the milk), *la torre* (the tower). In some cases, the ending of a word can provide clues as to which gender it is:

- Generally speaking, words ending in *-one (il melone* – the melon), *-ore (il colore* – the colour), *-ale (il canale* – the canal), *-ile (il cortile* – the courtyard) are masculine as are nounds ending in a consonant *(lo sport* – the sport, *il tram* – the tram).

- Nouns ending in *-ione (la stazione* – the station), *-ice (la lavatrice* – the washing machine), *-ie (la specie* – the type), *-aggine (la stupidaggine* – the stupidity), *-tà (la città* – the city) *and -tù (la gioventù* – the young people) are usually feminine.

■ Pluralization

The plural of nouns ending in *-o* and *-e* are formed by changing the final letter to *-i;* with nouns ending in *-a*, the final letter is changed to *-e*. Examples: *il ragazzo* – *i ragazzi, il cane* (the dog) – *i cani* and *la sculola* (the school) – *le scuole.*

Nouns ending in an accented vowel, *-tù* and *-tà*, as well ass those ending in a consonant have the same form in singular as in the plural; the pluralization is only apparent by the plural form of the article preceding the noun. Examples: *la virtù* (the virtue) – *le virtù, la città* – *le città, il film* – *i film, il tram* – *i tram.*

Adjectives

Adjective endings are determined by the gender and quantity of the noun or the person to which they refer, meaning a male would say *sono malato,* a female would say *sono malata,* and several people would say *siamo malati* (unless it is a group of women, then it is *siamo malate).*

There are adjectives ending in *-o* in the masculine form, *-a* in the feminine form or *-e* in both masculine and feminine, for example *nero* (black), *nera* and *grande*. The plural form of adjectives is formed as with the nouns; thus: *il cavallo nero* (the black horse) – *i cavalli neri* (the black horses), *la borsa nera* (the black purse) – *le borse nere* (the black purses), *la casa grande* (the large house) – *le case grandi* (the large houses).

As a general rule, adjectives follow the noun.

With some adjectives, the meaning is dependent on its position, for example *un negozio caro* (an expensive business) and *una cara amica* (a dear girlfriend), *un povero ragazzo* (a poor/pitiable boy) and *un ragazzo povero* (poor/moneyless boy).

■ Comparative Form

The comparative forms are created by adding *più* (= more): *bella/o* (beautiful) – *più bella/o* (more beautiful), *grande* (large) – *più grande* larger.

Declination

The declination in Italian takes on the form of prepositions *di* (of) combined with the articles *(il, lo, la);* in the genative case, this becomes *del, dello, della, dell'* in the singular form and *dei, degli, delle* in the plural form.
In the dative case this becomes *al, allo, alla, all'* for singular and *ai, agli, alle* for plural.

Examples:

la cattena del cane (the chain of the dog or the dog's chain), *la macchina dello zio* (the car of the uncle or the uncle's car), *la chiave della casa* (the key to the house), *vicino al fiume* (in the vicinity of the river), *scrivere dallo zio* (to write to the uncle), *scrivere alla zia* (to write to the aunt).
The accusative case is the same as the nominative case; thus: *vedo il ragazzo, la casa, i fiori etc.* (I see the boy, the house, the flowers etc.).

Pronouns

■ Personal Pronouns

The personal pronouns are *io* (I), *tu* (you, familiar), *lui* (he), *lei* (she), *noi (we), voi* (you, pl.), *loro* (they). These are, however, only used for special emphasis, for example *è stata lei,* (it was **she**) or *voi ci credete, noi no* (**you** (pl.) believe that, **we** don't).

■ Posessive Pronouns

The posessive pronouns are *mio* (my), *tuo* (your, familiar), *suo* (his, her), *nostro* (our), *vostro* (your, pl.), *loro* (their). These do change according to the gender of the noun.

Examples:

il mio (tuo, suo) libro – my (your, his/her) book
i miei (tuoi, suoi) libri – my (your, his/her) books
la nostra (vostra, loro) macchina – our (your pl., their) car
le nostre (vostre, loro) macchina – our (your pl., their) cars

■ **Pronouns used in Addressing People**

Like many other languages, the Italian has several forms of the second person. It is the third person singular when addressing an individual and the second (very formal) or third person plural when adressing a group. The personal pronouns in these cases are then capitalized when using this form: *Lei* and *Loro*.

When speaking to someone, one example of this form would be: *"(Lei) parla italiano?"* ("Do you speak Italian?") or *"(Lei) ha un passaporto?"* ("Do you have a passport?") and for more than one person: *"(Loro) parlano italiano?"* ("Do you (pl.) speak Italian?") or "*(Loro) hanno un passaporto?"* ("Do you (pl.) have a passport?"). In less formal situations, the *voi* form is used: *"(voi) parlate italiano?"* , *"(voi) avetet un passaporto?"*.

Verbs
■ The most important verbs (conjugations and tenses):

e s s e r e (to be) Present: *(io) sono* – I am *(tu) sei* – you (sing.) are *(lui, lei, Lei) è* – he, she is *(noi) siamo* – we are *(voi) siete* – you (pl.) are *(loro, Loro) sono* – they are	Future: *(io) sarò* – I will be *(tu) sarai* – you (sing.) will be *(lui, lei, Lei) sarà* – he, she will be *(noi) saremo* – we will be *(voi) sarete* – you (pl.) will be *(loro, Loro) saranno* – they will be

Past:
(io) ero – I was
(tu) eri – you (sing.) were
(lui, lei, Lei) era – he, she was
 	
(noi) eravamo – we were
(voi) eravate – you (pl.) were
(loro, Loro) erano – they were
	Conditional:
	(io) sarei – I would be
	(tu) saresti – you (sing.) would be
	(lui, lei, Lei) sarebbe – he, she
	              would be
	(noi) saremmo – we would be
	(voi) sareste – you (pl.) would be
	(loro, Loro) sarebbero – they
	              would be

Past Perfect: stato/a
(I have been – *sono stato/a;* you have been – *sei stato/a* etc.)

a v e r e (to have)

Present:	Future:
(io) ho – I have	*(io) avrò* – I will have
(tu) hai – you (sing.) have	*(tu) avrai* – you (sing.) will have
(lui, lei, Lei) ha – he, she has	*(lui, lei, Lei) avrò* – he, she will have
(noi) abbiamo – we have	*(noi) avremo* – we will have
(voi) avete – you (pl.) have	*(voi) avrete* – you (pl.) will have
(loro, Loro) hanno – they have	*(loro, Loro) avranno* – they will have

Past:	Conditional:
(io) avevo – I had	*(io) avrei* – I would have
(tu) avevi – you (sing.) had	*(tu) avresti* – you (sing.) would have
(lui, lei, Lei) aveva – he/she had	*(lui, lei, Lei) avrebbe* – he/she would have
(noi) avevamo – we had	*(noi) avremmo* – we would have
(voi) avevate – you (pl.) had	*(voi) avreste* – you (pl.) would have
(loro, Loro) avevano – they had	*(loro, Loro) avrebbero* – they would have

Past Perfect: *avuto*
(I have had – *ho avuto;* you have had – *hai avuto* etc.)

■ Verbs ending in *-are, -ere* and *-ire*
With these regular verbs, the various tenses for the individual persons I, you, he (she, it), we, you (pl.), they are conjugated in that the appropriate ending is added to the verb root. The following is one example for each of the three verb groups in the present tense:

p a r l a r e (to speak)	**c r e d e r e** (to believe)
(io) parl-o – I speak	*(io) cred-o* – I speak
(tu) parl-i – you (sing.) speak	*(tu) cred-i* – you (sing.) believe
(lui, lei, Lei) parl-a – he, she speaks	*(lui, lei, Lei) cred-e* – he, she believes
(noi) parl-iamo – we speak	*(noi) cred-iamo* – we believe
(voi) parl-ate – you (pl.) speak	*(voi) cred-ete* – you (pl.) believe
(loro, Loro) parl-ano – they speak	*(loro, Loro) cred-ono* – they believe

s e n t i r e (to feel, to hear, to percieve)

(io) sent-o – I feel   *(noi) sent-iamo* – we feel
(tu) sent-i – you (sing.) feel   *(voi) sent-ite* – you (pl.) feel
(lui, lei, Lei) sent-e – he/she feels   *(loro, Loro) sent-ono* – they feel

• Future Tense:
The verb root (like from *parlare, credere = parl-, cred-*) + *-erò, -erai, -erà, -eremo, -erete, -eranno* for the verbs ending in *-are* and *-ere.*
The verb root (like from *sentire = sent-*) + *-irò, -irai, -irà, -iremo, -irete, -iranno* for verbs ending in *-ire*

• Past Tense:
Verb root + *-avo, -avi, -ava, -avamo, -avate, -avano* for verbs ending in *-are* + *-evo, -evi, -eva, -evamo, -evate, -evano* for verbs ending in *-ere; + -ivo, -ivi, -ivamo, -ivate, -ivano* for verbs ending in *-ire*

The relaxing solitude of a beach on Sardinia

• Conditional Tense:

Verb root + *-erei, -eresti, -erebbe, -eremmo, -ereste, -erebbero* for the verbs ending in *-are* and *-ere*

Verb root + *-irei, –iresti, -irebbe, -iremmo, -ireste, -irebbero* for verbs ending in *-ire*

The Past Participle for the regular verbs ending in *-are, -ere* and *-ire* is formed by adding *-ato, -uto* and *-ito* to the root. In our examples, this would be *ho parlato* (I have spoken), *ho creduto* (I have believed), *ho sentito* (I have felt) etc.

The composite tenses are formed either:

• by using the auxilliary verb *avare* (to have) in conjunction with the past participle, whereby the participle remains unchanged *(ho avuto oggi la tua lettera* – I have received your letter today), or

• by using the auxilliary verb *essere* (to be) with the past participle, whereby the past participle is dependent on the gender and number of the subject *(lo zio è partito* – the uncle has departed, *la zia è partita* – the aunt has departed, *i genitori sono partiti* – the parents have departed, *le sorelle sono partite* – the sisters have departed).

The auxilliary verb *essere* is usually used for verbs designating motion or position.

Syntax and Negation
The Statement and the Question

Subject	Predicate	Object
Mio padre	*scrive*	*una lettera.*
My father	writes	a letter.

The inderect object then follows the direct object with "a"

Subject	Predicate	Object	Indirect Object
Mio padre	*scrive*	*una lettera*	*al professore.*
My father	writes	a letter	to the professor.

The syntax of the subject and predicate is reversed it the subject is to receive special emphasis:

Predicate	Subject	Object
Scrive	*mio padre*	*la lettera.*
My father writes the letter (and not my mother).		

Or in a question:

Predicate	Subject	Object
Scrive	*mio padre*	*la lettera?*
Does my father write the letter?		

The question can, however, also remain in the normal statement syntax:

Subject	Predicate	Object
I tuoi amici	*sono*	*in vacanza?*
Your friends	are	on vacation?

Negation
When negating a sentence, the word "non" is placed before the predicate:

Subject	Negation	Object
La mia amica	*non*	*viene?*
My girlfriend isn't coming		

The same is true for formulating questions both when using the inverted and the normal syntax.

The Basics

On the following pages are the most important phrases for any conversation no matter how basic. In addition, there are words that always come up like the time, numbers, colours, abbreviations and finally words and phrases having to do with the weather.

yes	Si	*see*
no	No	*noh*

Greetings

good morning/day	buon giorno	*bwon jornoh*
good evening/night	buona sera/notte	*bwohnah sehrah/nòteh*
hello/hi	ciao	*chow*
Mr/Mrs/Miss	signore/signora/ signorina	*sieeyoreh/sieeyorah/ seenyoreenah*

Introductions

My name is...	Il mio nome è mi chiamo ...	*il meeoh nohmeh eh/mee kyahmoh ...*
I come from ...	Sono di ...	*sohnoh dee ...*
What's your name, please?	Scusi, come si chiama?	*skuhzee, kohmeh see kyahmah?*
We phoned/We called.	Ci siamo sentiti al teléfono.	*chee syahmoh sentee-tee ahl telehfohnoh ...*
We made a reservation.	Abbiamo prenotato.	*ahbyahmoh prehnoh-tahtoh*

Give and Take

Excuse me, could you please tell me...?	Scusi, mi sa dire ...?	*skuhzee, mee sah deereh ...?*
I would like to ...	Vorrei ..., per favore	*vorehee..., pehr fahvoreh*
How much does that cost?	Quanto costa?	*kwahntoh kòstah?*

I would like to have...	Vorrei ...	*vorehee ...*
I need	Ho bisogno di ...	*oh beezònyoh dee ...*
Please give me...	Mi dia, per favore ...	*mee deeah, pehr fahvoreh ...*
Yes, please/no, thank you	Si/No, grazie.	*see/no, grahtsyë*
Not at all.	In nessun caso	*in nesuhn kahzoh*
I don't want to ...	Non vorrei ...	*nohn vorehee ...*
I don't want to anymore	Non ho più voglia.	*nohn oh pyuh volyah.*
I (don't) like it.	(Non) mi piace.	*(nohn) mee pyahcheh.*
I would most like...	Più di tutto mi piache-rebbe ...	*pyuh dee tuhtoh mee pyahcheh-rebeh ...*
rather than	Meglio ... che	*melyoh ... keh*
Thank you/thanks	Grazie	*grahtsyë*
Here you are	Prego	*prehgoh*
you're welcome	Non c'é di che	*nohn cheh dee keh*

Over the rooftops of Florence: at the centre, the calthedral with its baptistry

Smalltalk

Nice to meet you.	Piacere di conoscerLa.	*pyahtchereh dee konohshehrlah*
How are you?	Come sta?	*komeh stah?*
Where are you from?	Di dov'è?	*dee dohveh?*
I come from...	Sono di ...	*sohnoh dee ...*
How long will you stay?	Quanto tempo si fermerà?	*kwahntoh tempoh see fermehrah?*
Do you know the region well?	Conosce bene la regione?	*konosheh behneh la rehjohneh?*
Are you on holiday/vacation here?	E qui in vacanza?	*eh kwee in vahkahntsah?*
Are you here on business?	Viaggia per affari?	*vyahjah pehr ahfahree?*
Do you live here?	Abita qui?	*ahbeetah kwee?*
Where will you go on holiday/vacation?	Dove andrà in vacanza?	*dohveh ahndrah in vahkahntsah?*
How long have you been living here?	Da quanto tempo abita già qua?	*dah kwahntoh tempoh ahbeetah jah kwah?*
Can you recommend any special trip/sight to us?	Ci può consigliare una gita/qualcosa de vedere?	*chi pwoh konseelyahreh uhnah jeetah/kwahlkozah dah vehdereh?*
Are you familiar with America/Great Britain?	Conosce l'Amèrica/la Gran Bretagne?	*konosheh lahmehreekah/lah grahn brehtahnyë?*
Have you ever been to America/Great Britain?	E già stato/stata in Amèrica/Gran Bretagne?	*eh jah stahtoh/stahta in amehreekah/grahn brehtahnyë*
Could you please speak more slowly?	Può parlare più lentamente, per favore?	*pwoh pahrlahreh pyuh lentahmenteh, pehr fahvoreh?*
I don't understand.	Non capisco.	*nohn kahpeeskoh*
I don't speak very much Italian.	Parlo solo poco italiano.	*pahrloh sohloh pòkoh eetahlyahno*
Could you explain the word ... to me?	Mi può spiegare la parola ...	*mee pwoh spyehgahreh la pahrohlah ...*
What is this?	Che cosa è?	*keh kòsah eh?*
I am ... years old.	Ho ... anni.	*oh ... ahnee*
my boyfriend/girlfriend	il mio amico/la mia amica	*il meeyoh ahmeekoh/lah meeyah ahmeekah*

my husband/wife/ children/parents	Mio marito/mia moglie/i miei figli i miei genitori	*meeyoh mahreetoh/ meeyah molyeh/ee myehee filyee/ee myehee jeneetoree*
sister/brother	la sorella/il fratello	*lah sorelah/il frahteloh*
son/daughter	il figlio/la figlia	*il feelyoh/la feelyah*
Nice to have met you.	Piacere de averLa incontrato	*pyahchereh dee ahverlah inkontrahtoh*
Perhaps we'll meet again.	Forse un giorno ci rivediamo	*forzeh uhn jornoh chee reevehdyahmoh*
I am hungry/thirsty.	Ho fame/sete.	*oh fahmeh/seteh*
Cheers!	Cin cin/salute.	*chin chin/sahluhteh*
Enjoy your meal!	Buon appetito.	*bwon ahpehteetoh*
I have had enough.	Sono sazio/sazia.	*sohnoh sahtseeyoh/-ah*
beautiful/ugly	bello/brutto	*beloh/bruhtoh*
nice, kind/unfriendly	gentile/sgarbato	*jenteeleh/sgahrbahtoh*
interesting/boring	interessante/noioso	*interesahnteh/noyohsoh*

Good-bye's

Good-bye	Arrivederci	*ahreevehderchee*
Take care!/See you!	Auguri.	*owguhree*
Bye bye (familiar)	Ciao	*chow*
see you/so long	A presto	*ah prestoh*
'till (next) Monday	A lunedì (prossimo)	*ah luhehdee (pròseemoh)*

Pardon Me!

Excuse me, I'm sorry.	Scusi, mi dispiace	*skuhzee, mee dispyahcheh*

Numbers, Weights and Measures

Numbers from 1 to 1,000 and then some

0	zero	*dzehroh*
1	uno	*uhnoh*
2	due	*duheh*
3	tre	*treh*
4	quattro	*kwahtroh*

5	cinque	*chinkweh*
6	sei	*sehee*
7	sette	*seteh*
8	otto	*otoh*
9	nove	*nòveh*
10	dieci	*dyehchee*
11	undici	*uhndeechee*
12	dodici	*dohdeechee*
13	tredici	*trehdeechee*
14	quattordici	*kwahtordeechee*
15	quindici	*kwindeechee*
16	sedici	*sehdeechee*
17	diciasette	*deechasetteh*
18	diciotto	*deechotoh*
19	dicianove	*deechahnòveh*
20	venti	*ventee*

A magnificent portal in Venice

21	ventuno	*ventuhnoh*
22	ventidue	*venteeduheh*
23	ventitre	*venteetreh*
24	ventiquattro	*venteekwahtroh*
25	venticinque	*venteechinkweh*
26	ventise	*venteesehee*
27	ventisette	*venteeseteh*
28	ventotto	*ventotoh*
29	ventinove	*venteenòveh*
30	trenta	*trentah*
31	trentuno	*trentuhnoh*
32	trentadue	*trentahduheh*
40	quaranta	*kwahrahntah*
50	cinquanta	*chinkwahntah*
60	sessanta	*sesahntah*

In front of the Santa Maria sopra Minerva in Rome: if this elephant were real, it would be constantly stumbling over its trunk

70	settanta	*setahntah*
80	ottanta	*otahntah*
90	novanta	*nohvahntah*
100	cento	*chentoh*
101	cent(o)uno	*chent(oh)uhnoh*
105	centocinque	*chentohchinkweh*
150	centocinquanta	*chentohchinkwahntah*
200	duecento	*duhehchentoh*
300	trecento	*trehchentoh*
400	quattrocento	*kwahtrohchentoh*
500	cinquecento	*chinkwehchentoh*
600	seicento	*seheechentoh*
700	settecento	*setehchentoh*
800	ottocento	*otohchentoh*
900	novecento	*nòvehchentoh*
1,000	mille	*mileh*
1,001	milleuno	*milehuhnoh*
1,100	millecento	*milehchentoh*
1,150	mille centocinquanta	*mileh chentohchinkwahntah*
1,200	mille duecento	*mileh duhehchentoh*
1,900	mille novecento	*mileh nòvehchentoh*
2,000	duemila	*duhehmilah*
3,000	tremila	*trehmilah*
10,000	diecimila	*dyehcheemilah*
100,000	centomila	*chentohmilah*
1,000,000	un milione	*uhn milyohneh*
1,000,000,000	un miliardo	*uhn milyahrdoh*

More Number Words

first	il primo	*il preemoh*
second	il secondo	*il sekondoh*
third	il terzo	*il tertsoh*
fourth	il quarto	*il kwahrtoh*
fifth	il quinto	*il kwintoh*
sixth	il sesto	*il sestoh*
seventh	il settimo	*il seteemoh*

eighth	l'ottavo	*l'otahvoh*
ninth	il nono	*il nonoh*
tenth	il decimo	*il dehcheemoh*
eleventh	l'undicesimo	*l'undichehzeemoh*

The rule for forming the remaining ordinal numbers: the last letter in the word indicating the number is dropped and -esimo is added. One exception: the twenty-third = il ventitreesimo *(il venteetrehehzeemoh)*

once	una volta	*uhnah voltah*
twice/two times	due volte	*duheh volteh*
three times	tre volte	*treh volteh*

---

i **Weights and Measures**

Italians use almost exclusively grams and kilograms. In shops they purchase goods by the following weights: *un etto* (100 g), *due etti* (200 g), *un mezzo chilo* (500 g) or *un chilo* (1,000 g).

---

gram	il grammo (g)	*il grahmoh*
hectagram (100g)	l'etto (hg)	*letoh*
kilogram	il chilo (kg)	*il keeloh*
liter	il litro (l)	*il leetroh*
pound	il mezzo chilo	*il metsoh keeloh*
centimeter	il centimetro (cm)	*il chenteemehtroh*
meter	il metro (m)	*il mehtroh*
kilometer	il chilometro (km)	*il keelòmetroh*
dozen	la dozzina	*lah dodzeenah*

Currency

| the Italian Lira | La Lira Italiana (Lit.) | *lah leerah eetahlyahnah* |

Time

What time is it?	Che ora è?	*keh orah eh?*
It is one/two/three o'clock	è l'una/sono le due/ le tre ...	*eh luhnah/sohnoh leh duheh/leh treh ...*
It is half past twelve/one	sono le dodici e mezzo/è l'una e mezzo	*sonoh leh dohdeechee eh mehdzoh/eh luhnah eh mehdzoh*

It is a quarter to ...	è/sono ... meno un quarto	*eh/sohnoh ... mehnoh uhn kwahrtoh*
It is a quarter past ...	è/sono ... e un quarto	*eh/sohnoh ... eh uhn kwahrtoh*
It is three minutes to ...	è/sono ... meno tre minuti	*eh/sohnoh ... mehnoh treh meenuhtee*
It is three minutes past ...	è/sono ... e tre minuti	*eh/sohnoh ... eh treh meenuhtee*
(in the) afternoon	(il/di) pomeriggio	*(il/dee) pomereejoh*
(in the) morning	(la/di) mattina	*(lah/dee) mahteenah*
(at) noon/midday	(a) mezzogiorno	*(ah) medzohjornoh*
(in the) evening	(la/di) sera	*(lah/dee) sehrah*
(at) night	(la/di) notte	*(lah/dee) nòteh*
during the day	di giorno	*dee jornoh*
yesterday/today	ieri/oggi	*yehree/odjee*
(the day after) tomorrow	(dopo) domani	*(dòpoh) dohmahnee*
this morning	stamattina	*stahmahteenah*
tonight/this evening	stasera	*stahserah*
tomorrow evening	domani sera	*dohmahnee serah*
this week	questa settimana	*kwestah setteemahnah*
next week	la settimana prossima	*lah setteemahnah pròseemah*

Seasons, Months and Days of the Week

year	l'anno	*lahnoh*
spring	la primavera	*lah preemahvehrah*
summer	l'estate	*lestahteh*
autumn	l'autunno	*lowtunoh*
winter	l'inverno	*leenvehrnoh*
January	gennaio	*jenahyo*
February	febbraio	*febrahyo*
March	marzo	*mahrtsoh*
April	aprile	*ahpreeleh*
May	maggio	*mahjoh*
June	giugno	*juhnyoh*
July	luglio	*luhlyoh*
August	agosto	*ahgòstoh*

September	settembre	*zetembreh*
October	ottobre	*otohbreh*
November	novembre	*nohvembreh*
December	dicembre	*deechembreh*
Sunday	la domenica	*lah dohmehneekah*
Monday	lunedì	*luhnehdee*
Tuesday	martedì	*mahrtehdee*
Wednesday	mercoledì	*mercohlehdee*
Thursday	giovedì	*johvehdee*
Friday	venerdì	*venerdee*
Saturday	sabato	*sahbahtoh*
holiday	festivo	*festeevoh*
New Year's	capodanno	*kahpohdahnoh*
Easter	Pasqua	*pahskwah*
Christmas	Natale	*nahtahleh*

Advertising is everything — even in ancient times as can be seen from this sign for an ear doctor

> ### *i* Official Holidays in Italy
> Stores and banks remain closed for the most part on the following days:
> January 1, January 6 (The Three Magi), Easter Monday, August 15 (Mary's
> Ascention), November 1 (All Saints' Day), December 8 (Mary's Concep-
> tion) and on Christmas Day and Boxing Day.
> In addition, there are some holidays which are not related to the church:
> May 1 (Labour Day), April 25 (Day of Liberation), Republic Day falls on a
> Sunday (Festa Nazionale della Repubblica) on the first Sunday after June
> 2 and the Day of National Unity (Festa dell'Unita Nazionale) on the first
> Sunday in November.

The Date

Monday, October 23, 1993	lunedì, 23 ottobre 1993	*luhnehdee, venteetreh otohbreh milnòveh-chentohnòvahntahtreh*

Important Abbreviations

ACI = Automobile Club d'Italia	*owtohmohbeeleh klub deetahlyah*	Italian Automobile Club
AIG = Associazione Italiana Alberghi per la Gioventù	*asohcheeyahtsyohneh eetahlyahnah pehr lah joventuh*	Italian Youth Hostel Association
CAI = Club Alpino Italiano	*klub ahlpeenoh eetahlyahnoh*	*Italian Alpine Club*
CC=Carabinieri	*kahrahbeenyehree*	Italian police
CP=Codice Postale	*kohdeecheh pòstahleh*	P.O. Box
ecc. = eccetera	*ehcheterah*	etc.
ENIT = Ente Nazionale Italiano per il Turismo	*enteh nahtsyohnahleh eetahlyahnoh pehr il tuhreezmoh*	National Italian Tourist Office
E.P.T. = Ente Provinciale per il Turismo	*enteh prohveenchahleh pehr il tuhreezmoh*	Provincial tourist organisation
F.S. = Ferrovie dello Stato	*fehrohveeyeh deloh stahtoh*	National Italian Railway
Mitt. = Mittente	*mitenteh*	return address
P.S. = Pubblica Sicurezza	*publeekah seekurehtsah*	police
P.T. = Poste e Telecomuni-cazioni	*pòsteh eh tehlehkomuh-neekahtsyonee*	postal and telecom-munication system
S.I.P. = Società Italiana per l'esercizio Telefonico	*sohcheeyehtah eetahl-yahnah pehr lezehrchee-tsyoh tehlehfohneekoh*	Italian Telephone Company

TCI = Touring Club Italiano	_tuhring klub eetahlyahnoh_	Italian Touring Club
VV.UU. = Vigili Urbani	_veejeelee uhrbahnee_	municipal police

Colours

beige	beige	_behjeh_
black	nero	_nehroh_
blue	blu, azzurro	_bluh, adzuhrroh_
brown	marrone	_mahrohneh_
brown/dark (complexion, hair)/	scuro	_skuhroh_
green	verde	_verdeh_
grey	grigio	_greejoh_
light	chiaro	_kyahroh_
orange	arancione	_ahrahnchohneh_
purple	lilla	_leelah_
pink	rosa	_rohzah_
red	rosso	_rosoh_
white	bianco	_byahnkoh_
yellow	giallo	_jahloh_
colorful	colorato	_kolohrahtoh_
checkered	a quadretti	_ah kwahdretee_
striped	a strisce	_ah streesheh_
dotted	con puntini	_kòn punteenee_

The Weather

weather forecast	il bollettino meteorologico	_il boleteenoh mehtehorohl_ohjeekoh_
The weather is good/bad today.	Oggi è (fa) bel/ brutto tempo.	_odjee eh (fah) bel/ bruhtoh tempoh_
It is supposed to get better.	Migliorerà/peggiorerà	_meelyohrehr_ah/ pehjohrehr_ah_
warm/cold	caldo/freddo	_kahldoh/frehdoh_
sun/rain/ snow/drizzle	il sole/la pioggia/la grandine/la piog- gerellina	_il sohleh/lah pyohjah/ lah gr_ahndeeneh/lah pyohjereleenah_
fog/haze	la nebbia/la foschia	_lah nebyah/la fòsk_eea_

strong/moderate wind	il vento forte/debole	*il ventoh forteh/deboleh*
north/south/east/west	il Nord/il Sud/l'Est l'Ovest	*il nord/il suhd/lest/ lohvest*
storm/thunderstorm	la temtesta/il temporale	*lah tempestah/il temporahleh*
overcast/sunny	coperto/sereno	*kohpertoh/serehnoh*
partly cloudy	la schiarite	*lah skyahreeteh*
cold front/warm front	il fronte die aria fredda/calda	*il fronteh dee ahreeyah fredah/kahldah*
high/low pressure system/	la zona di alta/ bassa pressione	*lah dzohnah dee altah basah prehsyohneh*
fluctuating/variable	variabile	*vahreeyahbeeleh*
low/high tide	la bassa/l'aalta marea	*lah bassah/lahltah mahrehyah*
temperatures	le temperature	*leh tehmpeerahtuhreh*
degree Celsius	il grado celsius	*il grahdoh chelsyus*

At the Angel's Fortress: women of peace admire the historical weaponry

Travel and Transportation

Those driving a car will need the registration, proof of liability insurance and current proof of insurance in addition to a valid driving license. These must be presented upon request if stopped at traffic checkpoints. The car must also have a nationality sticker if entering Italy by car from another country; violaters are subject to a fine.

By Car

Roads and Streets

motorway/highway	l'autostrada	*lowtohstrahdah*
freeway/throughway	la superstrada	*lah suhpehrstrahdah*
one-lane	a una corsia	*ah uhnah korseeyah*
two-lane	a due corsie	*ah duheh korseeyë*
four-lane	a quattro corsie	*ah kwahtroh korseeyë*
road/street	la strada/ la via	*lah strahdah/lah veeyah*
(un)paved	(non) asfaltato	*(nohn) ahsfahltahtoh*
lane	il cammino	*il kahmeenoh*
oncoming traffic	il traffico in senso contrario	*il trahfieekoh in sehnsoh kontrahreeyoh*
one-way street	il senso unico	*il sensoh uhneekoh*
traffic circle	la circolazione rotario	*lah chirkohlahtsyohneh rohtahreeyoh*

Asking Directions

Excuse me, we've got a question.	Scusi/scusino (pl.) una domanda	*skuhzee/skuhzeenoh uhnah dohmahndah.*
We would like to get to ...	Vogliamo andare a ...	*vohlyahmoh ahndahreh ah ...*
Is this the road to ...?	Questa strada porta a ...?	*kwestah strahdah portah ah ...?*
How do we get to ...?	Come si arriva a ...?	*kohmeh see ahreevah ah ...?*

You have to turn back.	Bisogna tornare indietro	*beezònyah tornahreh indyehtroh*
This is the wrong way	Questa è la strada sbagliata	*kwestah eh lah strahdah sbahlyahtah*
This is the right way.	Questa e la strada	*kwehstah eh lah strahdah*
About how far is it?	Quanto è lontano all'incirca	*kwahntoh eh lontahnoh allinchircah*
Could you show us on the map?	Me/ce lo può indicare sulla carta stradale	*meh cheh loh pwoh indeekahreh suhlah kahrtah strahdahleh*
Could you speak more slowly, please?	Può parlare più lentamente	*pwoh pahrlahreh pyuh lehntahmenteh*
Could you repeat that, please?/pardon?	Può ripetere ancora una volta per piacere	*pwoh reepehtereh ahnkohrah uhnah voltah pehr pyahchehreh*
I didn't understand that.	Non ho capito	*nohn oh kahpeetoh*
(to the) right/left	a destra/sinistra	*ah dehstrah/ seeneestrah*
straight ahead	sempre diritto	*sehmpreh deereetoh*
after about a quarter of a mile	dopo 500 metri	*dópoh chinkweh chentoh mehtree*
intersection	l'incrocio	*linkróchoh*
traffic light	il semaforo	*il semahforoh*
curve	la curva	*lah kuhrvah*
(not) far	(poco) lontano	*(pòkoh) lontahnoh*
near	vicino	*veecheenoh*

The Most Important Road Signs

bad road	percorso cattivo	*pehrkorsoh cahteevoh*
caravan	roulotte	*ruhlòteh*
construction zone	cantiere	*kahntyehreh*
danger	pericolo	*pehreecohloh*
diversion/detour	deviazione	*dehveeyähtsyohneh*
do not block	lasciare libero il passaggio	*lashahreh leebehroh il pahsahjyoh*
do not enter	trànsito vietato	*trahnzeetoh veeyeh-tahtoh*
do not pass	senso proibito	*sensoh proheebeetoh*
exit	uscita	*uhsheetah*

falling rock	caduta sassi	*kahduhtah sahsee*
icy road	ghiaccio	*gyahchoh*
keep right/left	tenere la destra/sinistra	*tehnehreh lah dehstrah/seenistrah*
loose gravel/chippings	pietrisco	*peeyehtreeskoh*
no parking	divieto di parcheggio	*deevyehtoh dee pahrkehjyoh*
no stopping	divieto di sosta	*deevyehtoh dee sohstah*
no through traffic	transito vietato	*trahnzeetoh vyetahtoh*
one way	senso unico	*sehnsoh uhneekoh*
(parking) meter	parchimetro	*pahrk<u>ee</u>mehtroh*
passenger car	autovettura	*owtohvetuhrah*
pot-holes	buche	*buhkeh*
railroad crossing	passagio a livello	*pahsahjyoh ah leeveloh*
road constrution	lavori in corso	*lahvohree in korsoh*
road narrows	strettoia	*stretoyah*
slippery road	strada sdrucciolevole	*strahdah struhduh-chyohl<u>eh</u>vohleh*
slow	rallentare	*rahlehntahreh*
speed limit	limitazione della velocità	*leemeetahtsyohneh delah vehlohcheet<u>ah</u>*
stop	alt	*ahlt*
trailor	l'autocaravan	*lowtohkahrahvahn*
wet road/slippery when wet	strada umida	*strahdah uhmeedah*

Refuelling

service station	la stazione di servizio	*lah stahtsyohneh dee sehrveetsyoh*
Where is the nearest service station?	Dov'è il prossimo distributore di benzina?	*dohv<u>eh</u> il pr<u>ò</u>seemoh distreebuhtohreh dee behntseenah?*
fill it up, please!	Faccia il pieno, per favore	*fahchah il pyehnoh, pehr fahvoreh*
Check the oil.	controllare il livello dell'olio	*k<u>ò</u>ntrohlahreh il leevehloh del<u>oh</u>lyoh*
Refill the collant	rimettere l'acqua nel radiatore	*reemehtehreh lakwah nehl rahdyahtoreh*

Vocabulary: Service Station

car wash	l'impianto di autolavaggio	*limpyahntoh dee owtohlahvajoh*
diesel	il gasòlio	*gahzohlyoh*
fuel cap	il tappo del serbatoio	*il tahpoh del zehrbahtòyoh*
fuel pump	la colonna	*lah cohlohnah*
fuel tank	il serbatoio	*il zehrbahtòyoh*
nozzle	la pompa	*lah pòmpah*
petrol/gasoline	la benzina	*lah behndzeenah*
premium/four star	la (benzina) super	*lah (behdzeenah) suhpehr*
receipt	la ricevuta	*lah reechehvuhtah*
self-serve	self-service	*self-sehrvis*
tire pressure	la pressione delle gomme	*lah prehsyoneh deleh gohmeh*
unleaded	senza piombo	*sensah pyòmboh*

Car Trouble

Where is the nearest garage?	Dov'è la prossima officina?	*dohveh lah pròseemah ofeecheenah?*
The car won't start.	La macchina non va in moto.	*lah mahkeenah nohn vah in mohtoh*
Could you give me a tow?	Può rimorchiare la mia macchina?	*pwoh reemorkyahreh lah meeyah mahkeenah*
The tire is flat.	La gomma è sgonfia	*lah gohmah eh sgohnfeeyah*
front/back (rear)	avanti/dietro	*ahvahntee/dyehtroh*
right/left	a destra/a sinistra	*ah dehstrah/ah seeneestrah*
The engine is running hot.	Il motore si surriscalda.	*il mohtohreh see suhreeskahldah*
The engine is leaking oil.	La macchina perde dell'olio.	*lah mahkeenah pehrdeh delohlyoh*
The brakes don't work.	I freni non funzionano.	*ee frehnee nohn funtsyohnahnoh*
I don't know what's wrong.	Non so quale puó essere la causa.	*nohn soh kwahleh pwoh esehreh lah kowzah*

The battery is dead.	La batteria scarica.	*lah bahtehreeyah skahreekah*
Maybe there is something wrong with the plugs.	Forse le candele sono consumate.	*fohrseh leh kandeleh sohnoh kònsuhmahteh*
The exhaust pipe is defective.	Lo scappamento è guasto.	*loh skahpahmentoh eh gwahstoh*
I need new tires/ a new spare.	Ho bisogno di nuovi pneumatici/nuovo pneumatico di scorta.	*oh beezòhnyoh dee nwohvee nuhmahteekee/nwohvoh nuhmahteekoh dee skohrtah*
Can you repair this?	Lo può riparare?	*loh pwoh reepahrahreh?*
How long will it take?	Quanto tempo ci si vuole?	*kwahntoh tempoh chi see vwohleh?*
When can I pick up the car?	Quando posso venire a prendere la macchina?	*kwahndoh pòsoh vehneereh ah prehndehreh lah mahkeenah?*
Do you have the spare parts?	Ha dei pezzi di ricambio a disposizione?	*ah dehee petsee dee reekahmbyoh ah disposizsyohneh?*
How much will it cost?	Quanto costa?	*kwahntoh kòstah?*
Can you repair the part	Può riparare questo pezzo?	*pwoh reepahrahreh kwehstoh petsoh?*
Do you have to replace the part?	Bisogna cambiare il pezzo?	*beezòhnyah kahmbyahreh il petsoh?*

Automotive Anatomy

accelerator	il pedale dell'acceleratore	*il pehdahleh delachehlahtohreh*
axle	l'asse di supporto	*lahsseh dee suportoh*
battery	la batteria	*lah bahtehreeyah*
body	la carrozzeria	*lah kahròtdehreeyah*
bonnet/hood	il cofano	*il kohfahnoh*
boot/trunk	il portabagagli	*il pohrtahbagahlyee*
brake fluid	l'olio per freni	*lohlyoh pehr frehnee*
brake lining	la guarnizione del freno	*lah gwahrneetsyohneh del frehnoh*
brake pedal	il pedalo del freno	*il pehdahloh del frehnoh*
bumper	il paraurti	*il pahrah-urtee*

camshaft	l'albero a camme	*lahlbehroh ah kahmeh*
car radio	l'autoradio	*lowtohrahdeeyoh*
carburetor	il carburatore	*il kahrbuhrahtohreh*
catalytic converter	la marmitta catalitica	*lah mahrmitah kahtahleeteekah*
chassis	il carello	*il kahreloh*
clutch (pedal)	(il pedale della) frizione	*(il pehdahleh delah) freetsyohneh*
coolant hose	il conduttore dell'acqua del radiatore	*il kòndutohreh delah-kwah del rahdyahtohreh*
crankshaft	l'albero a gomiti	*lahlberoh ah gohmeetee*
dashboard	il pannello portastrumenti	*il pahneloh portahstruhmentee*
dimmer switch	il commutatore delle luci	*il kòmuhtahtoreh deleh luhchee*
door handle	la maniglia della porta	*lah mahneelyah delah portah*
door lock	la serratura della porta	*lah serahtuhrah delah portah*
exhaust pipe	lo scappamento	*loh skahpahmentoh*
fan	la ventilazione	*lah vehnteelahtsyohneh*
fog lights	il fendinebbia	*il fehndeenebyah*
front-wheel drive	la trazione anteriore	*lah trahtsyohneh ahntehreeyohreh*
fuel gauge	l'indicatore del livello della benzina	*lindeekahtoreh del leeveloh dela bendzeenah*
fuel tank	il serbatoio	*il sehrbahtoyoh*
fuse	il fusibile (valvola)	*il fuhseebeeleh (vahlvohlah)*
glove box/compartment	il cassetto del cruscotto	*il kahsetoh del kruskòtoh*
hazard warning lights	la spia (luminosa)	*lah speeyah (luhmeenohsah)*
heating	il riscaldamento	*il reeskahldahmentoh*
high-beams	la luce abbagliante	*lah luhcheh ahbahlyahnteh*
horn	il clacson	*il klahksòn*
ignition	l'accessione	*lahchehnsyohneh*
low-beams	la luce schermata	*lah luhche skehrmahtah*

oil pan	la coppa dell'olio	*lah kòpah del<u>oh</u>lyoh*
oil pump	la pompa dell'olio	*lah pòmpah del<u>oh</u>lyoh*
outside mirror	lo specchietto esterno	*loh spekyehtoh ehstehrnoh*
parking brake/handbrake	il freno a mano	*il frehnoh ah mahnoh*
parking lights	la luce di posizione	*la luhcheh dee pohseetsyoneh*
radiator	il radiatore	*il rahdyahtoreh*
radiator grille	la griglia del radiatore	*lah greelyah del rahdyahtoreh*
rearview mirror	il retrovisore	*il rehtrohveezoreh*
rear-wheel drive	la trazione posteriore	*lah trahtsyoneh pòstehreeyoreh*
rim	il cerchione	*il chehrkyohneh*
seat belt/safety belt	la cintura di sicurezza	*lah cheentuhrah dee seekuhrehtsah*
shock absorber	l'ammortizzatore	*lahmortidzaht<u>oh</u>reh*
spare wheel	la ruota di scorta	*lah ruhwohtah dee skortah*
spark(ing) plug	la candela d'accensione	*lah kahnd<u>eh</u>lah dahchentsyohneh*
speedometer	il tachimetro	*il tahkeemehtroh*
starter	il dispotivo d'avviamento	*il dispohteevoh dahvyahmentoh*
steering wheel	il volante	*il vohlahnteh*
steering wheel lock	il bloccasterzo	*il blohkahstehrtsoh*
stick shift/gear lever	la lev del cambio	*lah lehvah del kahmbyoh*
tire	il pneumatico/ la gomma	*il pnoimahteekoh/ lah gohmah*
transmission	il cambio	*il kahmbyoh*
turn signal	le freccie	*leh frecheh*
turn signal switch	il lampeggiatore	*il lahmpehjahtohreh*
warning light	la lampada di controllo	*lah lahmpahdah dee kòntròloh*
wheel	la ruota	*lah ruhwohtah*
windscreen/windshield	il parabrezza	*il pahrahbrehtsah*

| windscreen wiper/ windshield wiper | il tergicristallo | *il tehrjeekreestahloh* |
| wing/fender | il parafango | *il pahrahfahngoh* |

Vocabulary: Tools

angle iron/crowbar	il gomito	*il gohmeetoh*
brush	il pennello	*il peneloh*
cable	il cavo	*il kahvoh*
chisel	lo scalpello	*loh skahpeloh*
cross-head screwdriver	il cacciavite a croce	*il kahchahveeteh ah krohcheh*
drill	il trapano	*il trahpahnoh*
electric drill	il trapano meccanico	*il trahpahnoh mekahneekoh*
folding ruler	il metro	*il mehtroh*
glue	la colla	*lah kòlah*
hammer	il martello	*il mahrteloh*
hexagonal socket-head key	la chiave esagonale	*lah kyahveh ehzahgohnahleh*
hose	il tubo	*il tuhboh*
jack	il cricco	*il kreechoh*
jumper cables	il cavo di avviamento	*il kahvoh dee ahvyahmehntoh*
nail	il chiodo	*il kyohdoh*
nut	il dado	*il dahdoh*
pipe wrench	le pinze per tubi	*leh peentseh pehr tuhbee*
pliers	le tenaglie	*leh tehnahlyë*
pressure guage	il misuratore della pressione dell'aria	*il meezuhrahtohreh delah presyohneh delahreeyah*
rivet	il rivetto	*il reevehtoh*
sandpaper	la carta abrasiva	*lah kahrtah ahbrahseevah*
saw	la sega	*lah sehgah*
scissors	le forbici	*leh fohrbeechee*
screw	la vite	*lah veeteh*
screwdriver	il cacciavite	*il kahchahveeteh*

spanner/wrench	la chiave (per dadi)	*lah kyahveh (pehr dahdee)*
stripping knife	la spatola	*lah sp<u>ah</u>tohlah*
tool box	la cassetta portautensili	*lah kahsetah portah-uhtehnseelee*
tow rope	il cavo da rimorchio	*il kahvoh dah reemorhkyoh*
valve	la valvola	*lah v<u>ah</u>lvohlah*
wire	il filo	*il feeloh*

An Accident

There has been an accident.	E avvenuto un incidente.	*eh ahvehnuhtoh uhneencheedehnteh*
We had an accident.	Abbiamo avuto un incidente.	*ahbyahmoh ahvuhtoh uhn eenchidehnteh*
It is only light damage.	Ci sono solo danni alla carrozzeria.	*chee sohnoh sohloh dahnee ahlah kahr<u>ò</u>tsehreeyah*
I had to brake.	Ho dovuto frenare.	*oh dohvuhtoh frehnahreh*
He/She drove too close.	Si è avvicinato/a troppo.	*see <u>eh</u> ahveecheenah-toh/ah tr<u>ò</u>poh*
Please call an ambulance/ the police/ a doctor.	Chiami l'ambulanza/ la polizia/ un medico.	*kyahmee lahmbuhlahn-tsah/lah pohleetseeyah/ uhn m<u>eh</u>deekoh*
Could I see your driving licence?	La patente, per favore?	*lah pahtenteh, pehr fahvoreh?*
May I see your papers?	I Suoi documenti, per favore?	*ee swoyee dohkuh-mentee, pehr fahvoreh*
Did you see what happened?	Ha visto che cosa è successo?	*ah veestoh keh k<u>ò</u>zah <u>eh</u> suhchesoh?*
Could you act as a witness?	Può fare il testimone?	*pw<u>oh</u> fahreh il tehsteem<u>oh</u>neh?*
We will wait until the police arrive.	Aspettiamo finché arriva la polizia	*Ahspehtyahmoh feenk<u>eh</u> ahreevah lah pohleetseeyah*
It is not serious.	Non è grave	*Nohn <u>eh</u> grahveh*
Please give me your address.	Mi dia il Suo indirizzo, per favore	*mee deeyah il swoh indi-reetsoh, pehr fahvoreh*

| What is the name of your insurance company? | Quale è Sua assicurazione? | *kwahleh eh suhah ahseekuhrahtsyohneh?* |

Vocabulary: Accident

accident	l'incidente	*lincheedenteh*
ambulance	l'ambulanza	*lahmbuhlahntsah*
doctor	il medico	*il mehdeekoh*
first aid kit	la cassetta medica	*lah kahsetah mehdeekah*
help	l'aiuto	*lahyuhtoh*
injured persons	i feriti	*ee fehreetee*
police	la polizia	*lah pohleetseeyah*

Car and Motorcycle Rental

Where is the nearest car rental agency?	Dovè la prossima agenzia di noleggio di automobili?	*Dohveh lah pròseemah ahjehntseeyah dee nohlehjoh dee owtohmohbeelee?*
I would like to rent a car.	Vorrei noleggiare una macchina.	*Vorehee nohlejahreh uhnah mahkeenah*
How much is it per week/per day?	Quanto costa il noleggio per settimana/per giorno?	*kwahntoh kòstah il nohlehjoh pehr seteemahnah/pehr jornoh?*
Do you have a smaller/larger car?	Ha una macchina più piccola/ più grande?	*ah uhnah mahkeenah pyuh peekohlah/ pyuh grahndeh?*
Fill in the form.	riempire un modulo.	*reeyempeereh uhn mòduhloh*

Vocabulary: Car and Motorcycle Rental

car rental	l'agenzia di noleggio di automobili	*lahjehntseeyah dee nohlehjoh dee owtohmohbeelee*
comprehensive insurance	l'assicurazione con corpertura totale	*laseekuhrahtsyohneh kòn kohrpehrtuhrah tohtahleh*
damage	il danno	*il dahnoh*
deposit	la cauzione	*lah kowtsyohneh*
driver's license	la patente	*lah pahtehnteh*

exclusion of liability	l'esclusione di responsabilità	*lehskluhzyohneh dee rehspònsahbeeleet̲a̲h*
four-wheel drive	la transmissione su tutte le ruote	*lah trasmisyohneh suh tuhteh ruhwohtah*
helmet	il casco	*il kahskoh*
jeep/ off-road vehicle	il veicolo per marcia fuori strada	*il vehy̲e̲ekohloh pehr mahrchah fworee strahdah*
moped	il ciclomotore	*il cheeklohmohtoreh*
motor scooter	il motorino	*il mohtoreenoh*
motorcycle	la motocicletta	*lah mohtohcheeklehtah*
rental period	la durata del noleggio	*lah duhrahtah del nohlehjoh*
small car	l'utilitaria	*luhteeleetahreeyah*
unlimited mileage	il forfait chilometrico	*il fohrf̲e̲h keelohm̲e̲htreekoh*

By Train

Finding the Station

Where can I find the train station?	Dove si trova la stazione?	*dòveh see tròvah lah stahtsyohneh?*
How far is it to the (main) train station?	Quanto è distante la stazione?	*kwahntoh e̲h deestahnteh lah stahtsyohneh?*
Which bus/tram goes to the station?	Quale autobus/quale tram va alla stazione?	*kwahleh owtohbus/ kwahleh trahm vah ahlah stahtsyohneh?*

At the Station

Where can I buy a ticket?	Dove posso comprare un biglietto?	*dòveh pòsoh kòmprahre uhn beelyetoh?*
A ticket to ..., please.	Un biglietto per..., per favore	*uhn beelyetoh pehr..., pehr fahvoreh*
How much is a single/ return ticket to ...?	Quanto costa la corsa semplice/ andata e ritorno?	*kw̲a̲hntoh kòstah lah kòrsah sehmpleecheh/ ahndahtah eh ritornoh?*
Is there a student/ senior/children's discount?	C'è una riduzione per studenti/anziani/ bambini?	*ch̲e̲h uhnah reedutsyohneh pehr stuhdehnteh/ ahnzyahnee/bahm- beenee?*

I would like to reserve a seat.	Vorrei prenotare un posto/vorrei fare una prenotazione posti.	*vorehee prehnohtahreh uhn póstoh/vohrehee fahreh uhnah prehnoh-tahtsyohneh pòstee*
When does the next train leave/depart for ...?	Quando parte il pros-simo treno per..?	*kwandoh pahrteh il prò-seemoh trehnoh pehr..?*
From which platform does the train leave?	Da quale binario parte il treno?	*dah kwahleh binahreeoh parteh il trehnoh?*
Where can I check my luggage?	Dove posso deposi-tare i miei bagagli?	*dohveh pòsoh dehpòsi-tahreh ee myehee bagahlyee?*
I would like to send my bicycle ahead.	Vorrei spedire la mia biciletta in anticipo	*vohrehee spehdeereh lah meeah beecheekle-tah in ahnteecheepoh*
How much does it cost to send the bicycle to ...?	Quanto costa un biglietto per il transporto della bicicletta per...?	*kwahntoh kòstah uhn beelyetoh pehr il trahnspohrtoh delah beecheekletah pehr...?*
How soon do I need to drop the bicycle off?	Quanto tempo prima devo consegnare la bicicletta?	*kwahntoh tempoh pree-mah dehvoh kònsenyah-reh lah beecheekletah?*
I would like to pick up my luggage.	Vorrei andare a prendere i miei bagagli.	*vohrehee ahndahreh ah prehndehreh ee myehee bagahlyee*
Where is the baggaige claim?	Dove posso andare a ritiare i miei bagagli?	*dòveh pòsoh ahndah-reh ah reetyahreh ee myehee bahgahlyee?*
May I put my backpack here for a short while?	Posso deporre il mio zaino qua per un attimo?	*pòsoh depohreh il mee-yoh dzahyeenoh kwah pehr uhnahteemoh?*

In the Train

Is this seat free/taken?	E libero/occupato questo posto?	*eh leebehroh/òkuhpah-toh kwestoh pòstoh?*
All the seats are taken.	E tutto occupato.	*eh tutoh òkuhpahtoh*
There is a draft.	C'è corrente d'aria.	*cheh korehnteh dahreeah*
It is stuffy in here.	C'è aria pesante.	*cheh ahreeah pehzanteh*
Could you please close/ open the window?	Può chiudere/aprire la finestra?	*pwoh kyuhdehreh/ahpri-reh lah feenehstrah?*

May I put my suitcase/ backpack/bag here?	Posso porre la mia valigia/il mio zaino/ la mia borsa qua?	*pòsoh poreh lah mee-yah vahlijah/il meeyoh dzahyeenoh/la meeyah borsah kwah?*
Could you please help me lift my suitcase up here?	Mi può aiutare a sollevare la mia valigia?	*mee pwoh ahyuhtahreh ah sòlehvahreh lah meeyah vahlijah?*
Tickets please.	I biglietti, per favore.	*ee beelyetee, pehr fahvoreh*
Do you have a seat reservation?	Ha un biglietto di prenotazione?	*ah uhn beelyetoh dee prehnohtahtsyohneh?*
Where do I have to change trains?	Dove devo cambiare treno?	*dòveh dehvoh kahmbyahreh trehnoh?*
What is the next station/this station?	Come si chiama la prossima/questa stazione?	*kohmeh see kyahmah lah pròseemah/kwestah stahtsyohneh?*

A popular means of transportation in Venice: the gondola

Could you please tell me when I have to get out?	Mi dica, per favore, quando devo scendere?	*Mee deekah, pehr fahvohreh, kwahndoh dehvoh shendereh?*
we are delayed.	Siamo in ritardo.	*seeahmoh in reetahrdoh*
Will the connecting train to ... wait?	Aspettate la coincidenza per....?	*ahspetahteh lah koheencheedehntsah pehr....?*
Do not lean out.	non sporgesi	*nohn sporgehzee*

Vocabulary: Train Travel

arrival time	l'ora d'arrivo	*lorah dahreevoh*
centre	il centro	*il chehntroh*
compartment	lo scompartimento	*loh skòmpahrteemehntoh*
conductor	il controllore/la controllatrice	*il kòntrohlohreh/lah kòntrohlahtreecheh*
corridor	il corridoio	*il koreedoyoh*
couchette car	la carrozza con cuccette	*lah kahròtsah kòn kuhcheteh*
departure time	l'ora di partenza	*lorah dee pahrtehntsah*
dining car	il vagone-ristorante	*il vahgohnehreestorahnteh*
emergency brake	segnale d'allarme	*sehnyahleh dahlahrmeh*
vacant/occupied	libero/occupato	*leebehroh/òkuhpahtoh*
express train	il treno espresso	*il trehnoh espresoh*
first class	la prima classe	*lah preemah klahseh*
information	le informazioni	*leh infohrmazeeohneh*
lavatory	lavandino	*lavahndeenoh*
local train	il treno locale	*il trehnoh lohkahleh*
luggage counter	lo sportello accettazione bagagli	*loh sportehloh ahchetahtsyohneh bahgahlyee*
luggage locker	il deposito bagagli a cassette	*il dehpohzeetoh bahgahlyee ah kahseteh*
luggage rack	la rete portabagagli	*lah rehteh portahbahgahlyee*
platform	il marciapiede	*il mahrchahpyehdeh*
second class	la seconda classe	*lah sehkòndah klahseh*
sleeping car	il vagone letto	*il vahgohneh letoh*
stairs	le scale	*leh skahleh*

smoking/non-smoking	fumatori/vietato fumare	*fuhmatoree/veeehtahtoh fuhmahreh*
station restaurant	il ristorante della stazione	*il ristohrahnteh delah stahzeeohneh*
ticket	il biglietto	*il beelyetoh*
ticket check	il controllo biglietti	*il kòntrohloh beelyetee*
toilet	gabinetto/bagno	*gahbeenetoh/bahnyoh*
track	il binario	*il beenahreeyoh*
train car/wagon	la carrozza	*lah kahròtsah*
train schedule	l'orario	*lorahreeyoh*
wagon number	il numero della carrozza	*il nuhmehroh delah kahròtsah*
waiting room	la sala d'attesa	*lah sahlah dahtehstah*
window seat	un posto accanto al finestrino	*uhn pòstoh ahkahntoh ahl feenehstreenoh*

By Bus

Where is the bus terminal/bus stop?	Dovè la stazione/la fermata dell'autobus?	*dòveh lah stahdzyohneh/lah fehrmahtah dellowtohbus*
Where can I buy a ticket?	Dove compro i biglietti?	*dòveh kòmproh ee beelyetee*
Which bus goes to ...?	Quale autobus/quale linea va a ...?	*kwahleh owtohbus/kwahleh leenehah vah ah ...?*
Do you stop at/in ...?	Si ferma alla stazione ...?	*see fehrmah ahlah stahtsyohneh...?*
How long does the trip take?	Quanto dura la corsa?	*kwahntoh duhrah lah korsah?*
How much is the ticket?	Quanto costa il biglietto?	*kwantoh kòstah il beelyetoh?*
Do I have to validate the ticket myself?	Devo annullario io?	*dehvoh ahnulahryoh eeyoh?*

Vocabulary: Bus Travel

bus schedule	l'orario	*lorahreeyoh*
bus stop	la fermata	*lah fehrmahtah*
express bus	un autobus espresso	*uhn owtohbus espresoh*

intercity bus	l'autobus interurbano	*lowtohbuhs intehruhrbahnoh*
local bus	l'autobus urbano	*lowtohbuhs uhrbahnoh*
tickets	i biglietti	*ee beelyetee*

By Air

I would like to book a flight.	Vorrei prenotare un volo	*vorehee prehnohtah-reh uhn vohloh*
When is the next flight to ...?	Quando c'è un volo per...?	*kwahndoh cheh uhn vohloh pehr...?*
How much is the one-way/round-trip airfare?	Quanto costa il volo andata e ritorno?	*kwahntoh kòstah il vohloh ahndahtah eh reetornoh?*
When does the plane depart/arrive?	Quando parte/atterra l'aereo?	*kwahndoh pahrteh/ ahterah lahehrehoh?*
When do I have to be at the airport?	Quando devo arrivare all'aeropoto?	*kwahndoh dehvoh ahri-vahreh alehrohportoh?*
What is the flight number?	Qual'è il numero del volo?	*kwahleh il nuhmehroh del vohloh?*
Is the plane delayed?	E in ritardo l'aereo?	*eh in reetahrdoh lahehrehoh?*
How long is the delay?	Quando tempo è in ritardo?	*kwahndoh tehmpoh eh in reetahrdoh?*
Do I have a connecting flight to ...?	C'è la coincidenza per...?	*cheh lah koheenchee-dehntsah pehr...?*
I would like to continue on to ...?	Vorrei proseguire il volo per...	*vorehee prohsehgwee-reh il vohloh pehr..*
Where do I check my luggage?	Dov'è la spedizione bagagli?	*dòveh lah spehditsyoh-neh bahgahlyee?*
I would like to have this flight confirmed.	Vorrei fare confermare questo volo?	*vorehee fahreh kònfehr-mahre kwestoh vohloh?*

Vocabulary: Air Travel

airport	l'aeroporto	*lahehrohportoh*
connecting flight	il volo di coincidenza	*il vohloh dee koheencheedehtsah*
delay	il ritardo	*il reetahrdoh*
flight number	il numero del volo	*il nuhmehroh del vohloh*
gate	il gate	*il gahteh*

reservation/booking	la prenotazione/	*lah prehnotahtsyohneh/*
	la registrazione	*lah rehjeestrahtsyohneh*
return flight	il volo di ritorno	*il vohloh dee reetohrnoh*

By Ship

When does the next ferry/boat leave for ...?	Quando parte il prossimo traghetto/ la prossima nave per..?	*kwahndoh pahrteh il pròseemoh trahgetoh/ lah pròseemah nahveh pehr..?*
Where does the ferry/ boat depart?	Da dove salpa il traghetto/la nave?	*Dah dòveh salpah il trahgetoh/lah nahveh?*
How long does the trip last?	Quanto tempo durerà la corsa/il viaggio?	*kwahntoh tehmpoh duhrehrah lah korsah/ il veeyahjoh?*
How much is the ticket?	Quanto costa la corsa/il viaggio?	*kwahntoh kòstah lah korsah/il veeyahjoh?*
one-way/return	una corsa semplice /andata e ritorno	*uhnah korsah sehmplee- cheh/ahndahtah eh reetornoh*

Vocabulary: Ship Travel

deck passage	il passaggio-ponte	*il pahsahjoh-pònteh*
one-berth cabin	la cabina singola	*lah kahbeenah seengohlah*
passage/crossing	la corsa/il viaggio	*la korsah/il veeyahjoh*
ship	la nave	*lah nahveh*
two-berth cabin	la cabina con due letti	*lah kahbeenah kòn duheh letee*

By Bicycle

| Can I take my bicycle on the train? | E possibile spedire la mia bicicletta con il treno? | *eh pòseebeeleh speh- deereh lah meeyah beecheekletah kòn il trehnoh?* |
| How much is a bicycle ticket? | Quanto costa il biglietto per il transporto della bicicletta? | *kwahntoh kòstah il beelyetoh pehr il trahnsportoh delah beecheekletah?* |

Vocabulary: Bicycle

adhesive tape	il nastro adesivo	*il nahstroh ahdehzeevoh*
air pump	la pompa	*lah pohmpah*
axle	l'asse	*lahseh*
back pedal	il contropedale	*il kòntrohpehdahleh*
ball bearings	il cuscinetto a sfere	*il kuhsheenetoh ah sfehreh*
bike path	la pista ciclabile	*lah peestah cheeklahbeeleh*
brake	il freno	*il frehnoh*
brake shoes	il pattino del freno	*il pahteehoh del frehnoh*
cable	il cavo	*il kahvoh*
calliper brake	il freno sul cerchione	*il frehnoh suhl chehrkyohneh*
carrier	il portabagagli	*il pohrtahbahgahlyee*
chain	la catena	*lah katehnah*
cross-head screwdriver	il cacciavite a croce	*il kahchahveeteh a krohche*
cyclist	il ciclista	*il cheekleestah*
flat tire	il pneumatico sgonfio	*il pnoymahteekoh sgònfyoh*
fork	la forcella	*lah fohrchelah*
frame	il telaio	*il telahyoh*
front wheel	la ruota anteriore	*lah ruhwohtah ahntehreeyoreh*
gear shift	il cambio di velocità	*il cambeeyoh dee vehlohcheetah*
grease	il grasso per la catena	*il grahsoh pehr lah katehnah*
hammer	il martello	*il mahrteloh*
handlebar	il manubrio	*il mahnuhbreeyoh*
headlight	la luce anteriore	*lah luhcheh ahntehreeyoreh*
hub	il mozzo (della ruota)	*il mòtsoh (delah ruhwohtah)*
innertube	la camera d'aria	*lah kahmehrah dahreeah*
kick-stand	il posteggio	*il pòstejoh*

mudguard/fender	il parafango	*il pahrahfahngoh*
nut	il dado	*il dahdoh*
packing cord	le cinghie	*leh cheengyeh*
patent valve	la valvola	*lah vahlvohlah*
pedal bearing	il supporto dei pedali	*il supportoh dehee pehdahlee*
pedal brake	il freno contropedale	*il frehnoh kòntrohpehdahleh*
pedal	il pedale	*il pehdahleh*
puncture repair kit	il corredo per riparazione di forature	*il kòrehdoh pehr reepahratsyohneh dee forahtuhreh*
rain cape	l'impermeabile	*limpehrmeeyahbeeleh*
rear wheel	la ruota posteriore	*lah ruhwohtah pòstehreeyoreh*
reflector	il riflettore	*il reefletohreh*
rim	il cerchione	*il chehrkyoneh*
rivets	i rivetti	*ee reevetee*
saddle-bag	la sella	*lah sehlah*
screw	la vite	*lah veeteh*
screwdriver	il cacciavite	*il kahchahveeteh*
seat	la sella	*lah selah*
socket head key	la chiave esagonale	*lah kyahveh esahgohnahleh*
spokes	i raggi	*ee rahjee*
tail lights	la luce posteriore	*lah luhcheh pòstehreeyoreh*
ten-speed bicycle	la bicicletta a diece velocitá	*lah beecheekletah ah deeyehchee vehlohcheetah*
three-speed bicycle	la bicicletta a tre velocità	*lah beecheekletah ah treh vehlocheetah*
tire	il copertone	*il copehrtohneh*
valve	la valvola	*lah valvohlah*
wrench/spanner	la chiave (per dadi)	*lah kyahveh (pehr dahdee)*

Accommodation

In Italy, hotels are categorised according to the number of stars they are awarded. The price ranges for each category are determined by the government. One-star hotels are usually simple guest houses *(locande)* or inns. These also often serve dinner. Breakfast in Italian hotels is usually subject to an extra charge.

For those who look for accommodation on their own without advance reservations, the sign *"completo"* means that there are no more vacancies in the hotel.

Hotels and Guest Houses

Do you have any vacancies?	Ha ancora delle camere libere?	*ah ankohrah deleh kahmehreh leebreh?*
We reserved a room/ in writing.	Abbiamo prenotato una camera/ per iscritto.	*ahbyahmoh prehnoh-tahtoh uhnah kahmeh-rah/pehr iskreetoh*
a single/double (room)	una camera singola/ doppia	*uhnah kahmehrah seengohlah/dòpyah*
for two persons	per due persone	*pehr duheh pehrsohneh*
with a balcony	con balcon	*kòn bahlkohneh*
a child's bed	un letto per bambini	*uhn letoh pehr bahmbeenee*
running hot and cold water	l'acqua corrente calda/freddala	*lahkwah kòrenteh kahldah/frehdah*
radio/telephone/ television in the room	la radio/il telefono/ la televisione nella camera	*lah rahdeeoh/il telehfoh-noh/lah telehveezyoh-neh nelah kahmehrah*
for one night/two days/ a week	per una notte/due giorni/una settimana	*pehr uhnah nòteh/ duheh jornee/uhnah seteemahnah*
How much do you charge for the room?	Quanto costa la camera?	*kwahntoh kòstah lah kahmehrah?*
I'll take the room.	Prendo questa camera.	*prehndoh kwestah kahmehrah*

Do you have another room?	Ha ancora un'altra camera?	*ah ahnkorah uhnahltrah kahmehrah?*
I'll think it over.	Ci penso ancora.	*chee pehnsoh ahnkorah*
quietly situated/ at the back	tranquillo/che dà all'interno	*trahnkweeloh/keh dah ahlintehrnoh*
noisy/at the front	rumoroso/dà sulla strada	*ruhmorohsoh/dah suhlah strahdah*
Here is the key to your room.	Ecco la chiave della camera.	*ehkoh lah kyahveh delah kahmehrah*
If you go out, please leave the key at the reception.	Quando lasca la casa (l'albergo), consegni la chiave alla recezione.	*kwahndoh lahshah lah kahzah (lahlbergoh) kònsenyee lah kyahveh ahlah rehchetsyohneh*
Where is the bathroom/ the shower?	Dov'è il gabinetto/ la doccia?	*dòveh il gahbeenetoh/ lah dòchah?*
The tap is dripping.	il rubinetto dell'acqua gocciola.	*il ruhbeenetoh delah- kwah jòkohlah*

Camping with a view of the sea, for example on the Adriatic coast

The drain is clogged.	Lo scarico è intasato.	_loh sk**a**hreekoh **eh** eentahz**ah**toh_
The lightbulb is burnt out.	La lampadina si è rotta.	_lah lampahd**ee**nah see **eh** r**ò**tah_
switch/socket/light	l'interruttore/la presa/ la luce	_lintehr**u**toreh/lah pr**eh**zah/lah l**u**hcheh_
I would like to have an extra pillow/ blanket/towel.	Vorrei un'altro cuscino/ un'altra coperta/ altri asciugamani	_vor**eh**ee uhn**a**ltroh kush-**ee**nooh/uhn**a**ltrah koh-p**eh**rtah/ahltr**ee** ahshuh-gahm**ah**nee_
I have lost my key	Ho perso la mia chiave	_oh p**eh**rsoh lah m**ee**yah ky**ah**veh_
We would like to have breakfast in our room.	Vorremmo fare la prima colazione in camera	_vor**eh**moh f**ah**reh lah pr**ee**mah kohlatsy**oh**neh in k**a**hmehrah_
I/We will be leaving tomorrow at ... o'clock.	Partirò/partiremo domani alle...	_pahrteer**oh**/pahrteer**eh**moh dohm**ah**nee **a**hleh_
Could I have the bill, please?	Il conto, per favore	_il k**ò**ntoh pehr fah**vo**reh_

Vocabulary: Accommodation

air conditioning	l'aria condizionata	_l**a**hreeyah konditsy**o**h-nahtah_
balcony	il balcone	_il bahlk**o**hneh_
bathroom	il bagno	_il b**a**hnyoh_
bed	il letto	_il l**e**toh_
blanket	la coperta	_lah kohp**eh**rtah_
breakfast	la prima colazione	_lah pr**ee**mah kohlah-tsy**o**hneh_
chambermaid	la cameriera	_lah kahmehry**eh**rah_
child's bed	il letto per bambini	_il l**e**toh pehr bahm-b**ee**neh_
elevator/lift	l'ascensore	_lahchens**o**reh_
first floor	il primo piano	_il pr**ee**moh py**a**hnoh_
heating	il riscaldamento	_il reeskahldahm**e**ntoh_
hotel	l'albergo	_lahlb**eh**rgoh_
key	la chiave	_lah ky**ah**veh_
lavatory	il lavandino	_il lahvahnd**ee**noh_

luggage	i bagagli	*ee bahgahlyee*
pillow/head cushion	il cuscino	*il kusheenoh*
radio	la radio	*lah rahdeeoh*
reception	la recezione	*lah rehsetsyohneh*
reservation	la prenotazione	*lah prehnohtahtsyohneh*
second floor	il secondo piano	*il sehkòndoh pyahnoh*
shower	la doccia	*lah dòchah*
telephone	il telefono	*il tehlehfohnoh*
television/TV	il televisore	*il tehlehveezoreh*
third floor	il terzo piano	*il tertsoh pyahnoh*
toilet	il gabinetto	*il gahbeenetoh*
towel	l'asciugamano	*lahshuhgahmahnoh*

Other Accommodation

Do you rent out rooms?	Dà in affitto camere?	*Dah in affeetoh kahmehreh?*
private accommodations/ bed and breakfast	una camera privata	*uhnah kahmehrah preevahtah*
youth hostel	l'ostello della gioventù	*losteloh delah johventuh*
Youth Hostel ID	la tessera dell'ostello della gioventù	*lah tehsehrah delosteloh delah johventuh*
self-catering	cucinarsi da sè	*kuhchinahrsee dah seh*
kitchen	la cucina	*lah kuhcheenah*
dormitory	il dormitorio	*il dormeetoreeyoh*
we are looking for a campground.	Cerciamo un camping/campeggio.	*chehrkyahmoh uhn kahmping/kahmpehjoh*
How much do you charge per campsite?	Quanto costa il posto per la tenda/ /la roulotte?	*kwahntoh kòstah il pòstoh pehr lah tehndah/lah ruhlòt?*
adults/children	adulti/bambini	*ahduhltee/bahmbeenee*
What is your license plate number?	Qual'è il Suo numero di targa?	*kwahleh il swoh nuhmehroh dee tahrgah?*
Do you have a camping permit?	Ha una tessera di campeggio?	*ah uhnah tesehrah dee kahmpehjoh?*
How long do you plan to stay?	Quanto tempo rimarrà?	*kwahntoh tehmpoh reemahrah?*
Could we pitch our tent here/on your property?	Possiamo campeggiare sul Suo terreno?	*pòsyahmoh kampehjahreh suhl swoh terehnoh?*

Vocabulary: Camping

adults	gli adulti	*lyee ahduhltee*
batteries	le pile	*leh peeleh*
caravan/camper	la roulotte	*lah ruhlòt*
campground	il camping/	*il kahmping/*
	il campeggio	*il kahmpehjoh*
camping vehicle	l'autocaravan	*lowtohkahrahvahn*
camping permit	la tessera	*lah tesehrah*
	di campeggio	*dee kahmpehjoh*
camping stove	il fornello	*il forneloh*
car	la macchina	*lah mahkeenah*
children	i bambini	*ee bahmbeenee*
cooking facilities	il posto per cucinare	*il pòstoh pehr*
		kuhcheenahreh
dishes	i piatti	*ee pyahtee*
drain	lo scarico	*loh skahreekoh*
drinking water	l'acqua potabile	*lahkwah pohtahbeeleh*
dryer	l'essiccatrice/	*leseekahtreecheh/*
	l'asciugatrice	*lahshuhgahtreecheh*
flashlight/torch	la torcia	*lah torchah*
kerosine/paraffin	il petrolio	*il pehtrohlyoh*
rubbing alcohol/spirits	lo spirito	*loh speereetoh*
shower	la doccia	*lah dòchah*
silverware/cutlery	le posate	*leh pohzahteh*
sink	il lavello	*il lahveloh*
sleeping bag	il sacco a pelo	*il sahkoh ah pehloh*
tent	la tenda	*lah tehndah*
tent peg	il picchetto	*il piketoh*
tent pole	il palo da tenda	*il pahloh dah tehndah*
toilets	i gabinetti	*ee gahbeenetee*
washing mashine	la lavatrice	*lah lahvahtreecheh*
water canister	il bidone dell'acqua	*il beedohneh*
		delahkwah

Public Offices Banks and Telephone

The Police
Vigili Urbani is the local police force, concerned with ensuring law and order, enforcing parking regulations and also providing information. The *polizia (stradale)* is the traffic police. They stop those driving over the speed limit in addition to enforcing other traffic regulations. Traffic controls and public order fall under the jurisdiction of the *Carabinieri*. This is a special police force within the Italian armed forces (E.I.). The financial police, the *Guardia di Finanza* (G.D.F) are the customs officials. In addition to police and military responsibilities, their duties also include various tax and financial concerns.

Customs and Passport Control

Do you have anything to declare?	Ha qualcosa da dichiarare?	*ah kwahlkòsah dah deekyahrahreh?*
Your passport, please.	I Suoi documenti per favore.	*ee swoyee dòkuhmentee, pehr fahvohreh*
How many persons?	Quante persone siete?	*kwahnteh pehrsohneh syehteh?*
Do you have a visa/ insurance papers/ proof of vaccination?	Ha un visto/ una carta verde/ un certificato di vaccinazione?	*ah uhn veestoh/uhnah kahrtah vehrdeh/uhn chehrteefeekahtoh dee vahkeenahtsyohneh?*
Please open your suitcase.	Apra la valigia.	*ahprah lah vahleejah*
What is your destination?	Dove è diretto?	*dòveh eh deeretoh?*
How long do you plan on staying?	Quanto tempo rimarrà?	*kwahntoh tehmpoh reemahrah?*
What will you be doing in ...?	Che cosa intende fare a ...?	*keh kohsah intehndeh fahreh ah ...?*
I am on vacation/holiday.	Sono in vacanza.	*sohnoh in vahkahnzah*

Vocabulary: Customs/Passport Control

customs	la dogana	*lah dohgahnah*
identification/papers	documenti	*dòkuhmentee*
passport	il passaporto	*il pahsahportoh*
proof of vaccination	un certificato di vaccinazione	*uhn chehrteefeekahtoh dee vakeenahtsyohneh*
visa	un visto	*uhn veestoh*

Filling in Forms

Please fill out this form.	Riempa questo modulo.	*reeyehmpah kwestoh mòduhloh*
Sign here, please.	Firmi qua.	*feermee kwah*

Vocabulary: Forms

age	l'età	*leht<u>ah</u>*
citizenship	la nazionalità	*lah nahtsyohnahleet<u>ah</u>*
date (of birth)	la data (di nascita)	*lah dahtah (dee n<u>ah</u>-sheetah)*
date of entry/ departure	la data di entrata/ di uscita	*lah dahtah dee ehntrah-tah/dee uhsheetah*
date of issue	la data di emissione	*lah dahtah dee ehmisyohneh*
fees	la tassa	*lah tahsah*
first name	il prenome	*il prehnohmeh*
form	il modulo	*il mòduhloh*
last name	il nome	*il nohmeh*
maiden name	il nome da nubile	*il nohmeh dah nuhbeeleh*
place of birth	il luogo di nascita	*il lwohgoh dee nahsheetah*
place of issue (passport)	il luogo di emissione (del passaporto)	*il lwohgoh dee ehmi-syohneh (del pahsahportoh)*
place of residence	il luogo di residenza	*il lwohgoh dee reseedehntsah*
profession	la professione	*lah profehsyohneh*
signature	la firma	*lah feermah*

Money Matters

Where can I exchange money?	Dove posso cambiare soldi?	*dohveh pòsoh kahmbyahreh soldee?*
Where can I find a bank/currency exchange office?	Dove si trova una banca/un cambio?	*dohveh see trohvah uhnah bahnkah/uhn kahmbyoh?*
I would like to exchange 100 dollars/pounds into Lire.	Vorrei cambiare 100 dòllari/sterlina in Lire.	*vorehee kahmbyahreh chehntoh dohlahree/stehrleenah in leereh*
How many Lire do I get for 100 dollars/pounds?	Quante Lire avrò per 100 dòllari/sterlina?	*kwahntoh leereh ahvroh pehr chehntoh dohlahree/stehrleenah?*
Do you accept this credit card?	Accetta questa carta di credito?	*ahchetah kwestah kahrtah dee krehdeetoh?*
I would like to cash a traveller's cheque a Eurocheque.	Vorrei cambiare un'assegno turìstico/un eurocheque.	*vorehee kahmbyahreh uhnahsehnyoh tuhreesteekoh/uhn oyrohsheck*
What is the limit on this check?	Quanto posso prelevare al massimo con l'assegno?	*kwahntoh pòsoh prehlehvahreh al mahseemoh kòn lahsehnyoh?*

---

i Coins and Bank Notes

The Italian currency has been the Lira since 1862. There are coins in the denominations of L. 10, 20, 50, 100, 200 and 500. Bank notes of 1000, 2000, 5000, 10,000, 20,000, 50,000 and 100,000 Lire are in circulation. One and five Lire coins are no longer in circulation.

Vocabulary: Money Matters

account	il conto	*il kòntoh*
cash	il denaro contante	*il dehnahroh kòntahnteh*
check card	la carta assegni	*lah kahrtah ahsehnyee*
check	l'assegno	*lahsehnyoh*
commission	i diritti dell'assegno/la spese bancarie	*ee deeritee delahsehnyoh/lah spehseh bahnkahreeyeh*
credit card	la carta di credito	*lah kahrtah dee krehditoh*

Local Authorities

Where is the nearest police station?	Dov'è il prossimo distretto di polizia?	*dòveh il pròseemoh deestrehtoh dee pohleetseeyah?*
I have lost my passport.	E sparito il mio passaporto.	*eh spahreetoh il meeyoh pahsahportoh*
My car has been broken into.	Hanno forzato la mia macchina.	*ahnnoh fortsahtoh lah meeyah mahkeenah*
My purse/passport/ wallet has been stolen.	Mi hanno rubato la borsa/il passaporto /la carta assegni.	*mee ahnoh ruhbahtoh lah borsah/il pahsah-portoh/lah kahrtah ahsehnyee*
My (traveller's) checks have been stolen.	Mi hanno rubato gli assegni (turìstico).	*mee ahnoh ruhbahtoh lyee ahsehnyee (tureesteekoh*
I would like to file a report.	Vorrei presentare una denuncia.	*vorehee prehsentahreh uhnah dehnunchah*

The massive dome of St. Peter's Cathedral in Rome rises above a sea of houses

Could you register a report for me?	Può fare un verbale?	*pwoh fahreh uhn vehrbahleh*'?
I have lost my (traveller's) checks/passport/wallet.	Ho perso i miei assegni (turistichi)/ il passaporto.	*oh pehrsoh ee myehee ahsehnyee (tuhreestee kee)/il pahsahportoh*
Where can I find the British/American embassy?	Dove si trova l'ambasciata bri- tànnico/americano?	*doveh see trovah lahm- bahshahtah breetahnee- koh/ahmehreekahnoh?*

---

i Tips for the public telephone in Italy

Calls can be placed in hotels (but this usually involves a surcharge), in many bars (these display a yellow sign with a black dial outside) or in telephone booths. To place a call, one can use either coins (100, 200 or 500 Lire) or *gettoni* (special telephone tokens) with a value of 200 Lire; these can be purchased in bars and tobacco shops. Another option is the telephone card *(carta telefonica)* with a value of 5000 or 10,000 Lire; these are available at the S.I.P. offices, the private Italian telephone company. The best option for placing longer international calls is with the telephone cards. S.I.P. offices are open from 7 am to 10 pm. Discounted telephone rates include: 30% discount Monday to Friday from 6:30 to 10 pm; Saturdays from 1 to 10 pm 50% every day from 10 pm to 8 am. The international code for calls to the United Kingdom is 0044; to the United States, 001 followed by the area code.

Where is the nearest public telephone?	Dov'è la prossima cabina telefonica?	*dohveh lah pròseemah kahbeenah telehfoh neekah?*
Could you give me change?	Mi può cambiare questo in spiccioli?	*mee pwoh kahmbyahreh kwestoh in spichohlee?*
I would like to place a call to Great Britain/ the United States.	Vorrei telefonare in Inglterra/Amèrica.	*vorehee telehfohnahreh in inglahtehrah/ ahmehreekah*
Which booth?	Quale cabina è?	*kwahleh kahbeenah eh?*
Can I dial direct?	Si può telefonare direttamente?	*see pwoh telehfohahreh deeretahmenteh?*
I would like to place a collect call.	Vorrei fare una telefonata R.	*vorehee fahreh uhnah telehfohnahtah ehreh*
My name is ...	Mi chiamo/ il mio nome è...	*mee kyahmoh/il meeyoh nohmeh eh ...*

May I speak to Mr./Mrs. ...	Posso parlare con il signore/la signora...?	*pòsoh pahrlahreh kòn il seenyohreh/lah seenyohrah ...?*
With whom am I speaking?	Con chi parlo, per favore?	*kòn kee pahrloh pehr fahvoreh?*
... is not here right now.	... non è a casa.	*... nohn eh ah kahzah*
The line is busy/engaged.	il telefono è occupato.	*il telehfohnoh eh òkuhpahtoh*
May I call again later?	Posso richiamare più tardi?	*pòsoh reekyahmahreh pyuh tahrdee?*
Please hold the line.	Rimanga in linea.	*reemahngah in leenehah*
One moment please.	Aspetti un attimo.	*ahspetee uhn ahteemoh*
I would like to send a telegram	Vorrei spedire un telegramma.	*vorehee spehdeereh uhn telehgrahmah*
How much does a telegram to ... cost?	Quanto costa un telegramma per ...?	*kwahntoh kòstah uhn telehgrahmah pehr ...?*
per word	per/a parola	*pehr/ah pahrohlah*

Vocabulary: Telephone

area/trunk code	il prefisso telefonica	*il prehfisoh telehfohneekoh*
charges	lo scatto	*loh skahtoh*
collect call	la telefonata R	*lah telehfohnahtah ehreh*
country code	il prefisso nazionale	*il prehfisoh nahtsyohnahleh*
information	le informazioni telefoniche	*leh informahtsyohnee telehfohneekeh*
interference	il guasto	*il gwahstoh*
operater	la centrale telefonica	*lah chentrahleh telehfohneekah*
payphone/phone booth	la cabina telefonica	*lah kahbeenah telehfohneekah*
phone number	il numero dell'abbonato	*il nuhmehroh delahbohnahtoh*
phonebook	l'elenco telefonico	*lelehnkoh telehfohneekoh*

| yellow pages | l'elenco telefonico per categorie/le pagine gialle | *lelehnkoh telehf<u>oh</u>nee-koh pehr kahtehgohree-yeh/lah p<u>ah</u>jeeneh jahleh* |

The Italian Spelling Alphabet

A = Ancona	*ahnkohnah*	N = Napoli	*nahpohlee*
B = Bologna	*bòlònyah*	O = Otranto	*òtrahntoh*
C = Como	*kohmoh*	P = Padova	*pahdohvah*
D = Domodossola	*dohmoh-dòsohlah*	Q = Quarto	*kwahrtoh*
E = Empoli	*<u>eh</u>mpohlee*	R = Roma	*rohmah*
F = Firenze	*feerentseh*	S = Savona	*sahvohnah*
G = Genova	*j<u>eh</u>nohvah*	T = Torino	*toreenoh*
H = Hotel	*ohtel*	U = Undine	*uhdeeneh*
I = Imola	*<u>ee</u>mohlah*	V = Venezia	*ven<u>eh</u>tsyah*
J = Jersey	*jersee*	W = Washington	*wòshington*
K = Kursaal	*kuhrsahl*	X = Xeres	*ksehrehz*
L = Livorno	*leevornoh*	Y = York	*york*
M = Milano	*meelahnoh*	Z = Zara	*dzahrah*

Cuisine and Dining Out

Those who visit a *Trattoria* or *Ristorante* should at least order a starter *(antipasto)* and a main course. Usually, one orders two courses *(primo* and *secondo piatto)* to follow the appetizer. It is frowned upon if one orders only a pizza or pasta dish. Another difference in Italy is that a surcharge is added to the bill for the cover *(coperto)*.

Restaurants

Could you recommend a good restaurant?	Mi può raccomandare un buon ristorante?	*mee pwoh rahkohmahn-dahreh uhn bwohn reestorahnteh?*
Is there a good and inexpensive restaurant nearby?	C'è qua un ristorante buono e a prezzo conveniente?	*cheh kwah uhn reesto-rahnteh bwohnoh eh ah pretsoh konvehnyenteh?*
Do you need reservations?	Bisogna prenotare un tavolo?	*beezònyah prehnoh-tahreh uhn tahvohloh?*
I would like to reserve a table for ... persons for tonight.	Vorrei prenotare un tavolo per...persone per stasera.	*vorehee prehnohtahreh uhn tahvohloh pehr...pehrzohneh pehr stahsehrah*
Is this seat taken?	E ancora libero questo posto?	*eh ahnkorah leebehroh kwestoh pòstoh?*
The menu, please.	La lista, per favore.	*lah leestah, pehr fahvoreh*
Have you already chosen?	Ha già deciso?	*ah jah dehcheezoh?*
Would you like an aperitif?	Prende un aperitivo?	*prendeh uhnahpehree-teevoh?*
What may I bring you?	Che cosa Le posso portare/portare Loro (pl.)?	*keh kòzah leh pòsoh portahreh/portahreh loroh?*
What would you like to drink?	Che cosa desidera/desiderano (pl.) mangiare/bere?	*keh kòzah dehzeederah/dehzeederahnoh mahn-jahreh/behreh?*

What would you like as an appetizer/starter first\second course?	Che antipasto/primo/ secondo piatto prende/ prendono (pl.)?	*keh ahnteepahstoh/pree-moh/sehkòndoh pyahtoh prendeh/prendohnoh?*
I'd like ...	Io prendo ...	*eeoh prendoh ...*
a glass of ... beer/wine/juice/ mineral water	un bicchiere ... di birra/di vino/di succo di frutta/ di acqua minerale	*uhn beekyehreh ... dee beerah/veenoh/dee zukoh dee frutah/dee ahkwah meenehrahleh*
rosé/red/white wine	di rosato/vino rosso/ vino bianco	*dee rohzahtoh/veenoh ròsoh/veenoh byahnkoh*
I did not order this.	Non ho ordinato questo.	*nohn oh ordeenahtoh kwestoh*
I need a knife/fork/spoon/ another plate/a glass.	Ho bisogno di un coltello/una forchetta/ un cucchiaino/un altro piatto/un bicchiere.	*oh beezònyoh dee uhn kolteloh/uhnah forketah/ uhn kuhchyaheenoh/uh-ahltroh pyahttoh/uhn bikyehreh*
Did you enjoy your meal?	E piaciuto?	*eh pyahchuhtoh?*

Dining outside on the Piazza Navona in Rome

The meal was delicious/ very good/too salty.	Era eccellente/buonis-simo/troppo salato.	*ehrah ehchehlenteh/ bwohneeseemoh/tròpoh sahlahtoh*
The meat was tough.	La carne era dura.	*lah kahrneh ehrah durah*
Will there be anything else?	Desidera altro?	*dehzeedehrah ahltroh?*
I would like a cup/pot of tea/coffee/hot chocolate.	Vorrei una tazza/un bricchetto di tè/cafè/ cioccolata.	*vorehee uhna tahdzah/ uhn breeketoh dee teh/ kahfeh/chòkohlahtah*
What yould you like for dessert?	Che desert/dolce prende/prendono (pl.)?	*keh dehzehr/dòlcheh prendeh/prendonoh?*
I would like a pastry/ piece of cake /pie.	Vorrei un pezzo di torta/dolce/torta di frutta.	*vorehee uhn petsoh dee tortah/dòlcheh/tortah dee frutah*
The bill, please.	Il conto, per favore.	*il kòntoh, pehr fahvoreh*
One bill/separate bills, please.	Paghiamo insieme/ ognuno per conto proprio (pagare alla romana).	*pahgyahmoh insyehmeh/ onyuhnoh pehr kòntoh prohpreeyoh (pahgah-reh ahlah rohmahnah)*
VAT/service included	IVA (imposata sul valore aggiunto)/ servizio incluso	*eevah (impohsahtah suhl vahloreh ajuntoh)/ sehrveetsyoh inkluhzoh*
Where are the restrooms/toilets?	Dove si trova il bagno/si trovano i gabinetti?	*dohveh see trohvah il bahnyoh/see trohvah-noh ee gahbeenetee?*
ladies/men	donne/uomini	*dòneh/wohmeenee*

Vocabulary: Dining Out

appetizer/starter	l'antipasto	*lahnteepahstoh*
beer	la birra	*lah beerah*
beverages	le bevande	*lah behvahndeh*
bill	il conto	*il kòntoh*
boiled	bollito	*bòleetoh*
breakfast	la prima colazione	*lah preemah kohlahtsyohneh*
coffee	il caffè	*il kahfeh*
cup	una tazza	*uhna tahtsah*
dessert	il dessert/il dolce	*il dehsehr/il dòlcheh*
dinner/supper	la cena	*lah chehnah*
fish dishes	il pesce	*il pesheh*

fork	la forchetta	*lah forketah*
fried	arrosto	*ahrohstoh*
fruit	la frutta	*lah frutah*
glass	il bicchiere	*il beekyehreh*
grilled	alla griglia	*ahlah greelyah*
hot chocolate	cioccolata	*chòkohlahtah*
juice	il succo di frutta	*il sukoh dee frutah*
juice, fresh squeezed	la spremuta di ...	*lah sprehmuhtah dee ...*
knife	il coltello	*il kohtelloh*
lunch	il pranzo	*il prahndzoh*
main course	il primo/secondo piatto	*il preemoh/sehkòndoh pyahtoh*
meat dishes	la carne	*lah kahrneh*
medium	non cotto	*nohn kòtoh*
menu	la lista	*lah leestah*
mineral water	l'acqua minerale	*lahkwah meenehrahleh*
noodles/pasta	le paste	*leh pahsteh*
pastries	i biscotti	*ee beeskòtee*
place setting/cover	il coperto	*il kohpehrtoh*
plate	il piatto	*il pyahtoh*
rare	poco cotto, al sangue	*pohkoh kòtoh, ahl sahngweh*
raw	crudo	*kruhdoh*
seafood	i frutti di mare	*ee frutee dee mahreh*
service	il servizio	*il sehrveetsyoh*
silverware/cutlery	le posate	*leh pòstahteh*
snack	la qualcosa	*lah kwahlkòzah*
soup	la zuppa	*lah dzupah*
sour	acido	*acheedoh*
steamed	stufato	*stuhfahtoh*
sweet	dolce	*dòlcheh*
tablespoon	il cucchiaio	*il kukyahyoh*
tea	il tè	*il teh*
teaspoon	il cucchiaino	*il kùkyaheenoh*
vegetables	le verdure	*leh vehrduhreh*
waiter/waitress	il cameriere/ la cameriera	*il kahmehryehreh/ lah kahmehryehrah*

water (with ice)	l'acqua (fredo)	*lahkwah (frehdoh)*
well done	ben cotto	*behn kòtoh*
wine	il vino	*il veenoh*

Other Options

snack bar	la tavola calda	*lah tahvohlah kahldah*
café/bar	il caffè, il bar	*il kahfeh, il bar*
tearoom	il salone da tè	*il sahlohneh dah teh*
pub	la trattoria	*lah trahtohreeyah*

The Menu

Starters/Appetizers (antipasti)

il pane	*il pahneh*	bread
i panini	*ee pahneenee*	rolls
grissini	*griseenee*	breadsticks
salame	*sahlahmeh*	sausage/coldcuts

A true classic among Italian pasta dishes: spaghetti with spicy garlic sauce

salsiccia	*sahlseechah*	sausages
prosciutto crudo/	*prohshuhtoh kruhdoh*	cured ham
prosciutto cotto	*prohshuhtoh kòtoh*	cooked ham
pancetta	*pahnchetah*	pork belly
affettato	*ahfetahtoh*	sausage slices/coldcuts

Soups (zuppe)

brodo/consomé	*brohdoh/konsohmeh*	broth/beef broth
minestra	*meenehstrah*	soup with sausage
minestrone	*meenehstrohneh*	thick vegetable soup
stracciatella	*strahchahtelah*	beef broth with egg

Primo Piatto (first main dish)

risotto	*reesòtoh*	rice dish
polenta	*pohlentah*	corn flour cakes
pizza	*peedza*	pizza

Italian pasta dishes are famous the world over, like penne with ham and olives

Pasta

Pasta is the Italian national dish, served as the first of two main courses; thus, *primo piatto* (first course) following the actual appetizer *(antipasto)*. Pasta is served *al dente* and there are both fresh and dried pastas *(pasta fresca* and *pasta secca)*. *Pastaciutta* (= dry pasta) means it is prepared with sauce or ragout in contrast to *pasta in brodo* (pasta in broth). *Pasta lunga* are long noodles which are either round like the thin *capellini, vericelli* and *spaghettini* as well as the thicker *spaghetti*, or flat ranging from the slender *linguine* and *bavette* to t*agliatelle, fettuccine* or *fettuce* all the way to the broad *lasagne*. There are also nudels shaped into a "nest" like t*aglioni, barbine, tagliatelle* and *fettuchine)* or with a hole in the centre called *con buco (bucatini, cannelloni, maccheroni, ziti)*. *Pasta corta* are short noodles with a hole in the middle like *ditali, penne, rigatoni* and *sedani*. Pasta with a special form include *conchiglie* (shell shaped), *eliche* (spiral shaped), *farfalle* (butterfly shaped), *risoni* (in the form of rice) and *stelline* (star shaped). Pasta with a filling *(pasta ripiena)* inlcudes *agnolotti, ravioli, tortellli, tortellini* and *tortelloni*. The filling is made from meat, bread crunbs, grated cheese, spices or even *ricotta* cheese.

Fish and Seafood

acciuge	*ahchuhgeh*	anchovies
anguilla	*ahngweelah*	eel
aragosta	*ahrahgòstah*	lobster
aringa	*ahreengah*	herring
baccalà	*bahkahl<u>ah</u>*	stockfish, dried cod
calamari	*kahlahmahree*	cuttlefish/octopus
carpa	*kahrpah*	carp
cefalo	*ch<u>e</u>hfahloh*	mullet
cernia	*ch<u>e</u>hrneeyah*	saw-fish
cozze	*kòtseh*	mussels
datteri	*d<u>a</u>htehree*	date mussels
dentice	*dehnteecheh*	bream
fritto misto	*fritoh mistoh*	mixed, deep-fried fish and seafood
gamberetti/ granchi	*gahmbehretee/ grahnkee*	shrimps
gambero	*gahmbehroh*	crab
gambero di mare	*gahmbehro dee mahreh*	lobster
gamberoni	*gahmbehrohnee*	prawns
luccio	*luhchoh*	pike

merluzzo	_mehrlutsoh_	sea pike
nasello	_nahzeloh_	haddock
orata	_orahtah_	golden shiner (bream)
ostriche	_òstreekeh_	oysters
pescatrice	_peskahtreecheh_	devilfish/ray
pesce persico	_pesheh pehrzeekoh_	perch
pesce spada	_pesheh spahdah_	swordfish
pesce ragno	_pesheh rahnyoh_	sea perch
polpo	_pòlpoh_	polyp
razza	_rahtsah_	ray
riccio mario	_reechoh mahreenoh_	sea urchin
rombo	_ròmboh_	turbot
salmone	_sahlmohneh_	salmon
sarde	_sahrdeh_	sprats
sardine	_sahrdeeneh_	sardines
scampi	_skahmpee_	jumbo shrimps
sgombro	_sgòmbroh_	mackerel
sogliola	_sohlyohlah_	sole
storione	_storyohneh_	sturgeon
tonno	_tònoh_	tuna/tunny
triglia	_treelyah_	sea barbel
trota	_trohtah_	trout
vongole	_vongohleh_	small, light mussels
zuppa di pesce	_dzupah dee pesheh_	fish soup
lumache	_luhmahkeh_	snails/escargots
rane	_rahneh_	frogs' legs

Meats

agnello/abbacchio	_ahnyeloh/ahbakyoh_	lamb/milk-fed lamb
bue	_buheh_	ox
capretto	_kahpretoh_	young goat
coniglio	_kòneelyoh_	rabbit
maiale	_mahyahleh_	pork
manzo	_mahndzoh_	beef
montone	_mòntohneh_	mutton
porchetto	_porketoh_	suckling pig
vitello	_veeteloh_	veal

vitellone	*veetelohneh*	young beef

Cuts of Meat

bistecca	*bistekah*	steak
cervello	*chehrveloh*	brains
coda	*kohdah*	tail
coscia (di vitello)	*kòshah (dee veeteloh)*	leg (of veal)
cuore	*kworeh*	heart
costata	*kòstahtah*	cutlet
fegato	*fehgahtoh*	liver
lingua	*leengwah*	tongue
lombata	*lohmbahtah*	fillet, tenderloin
ossobuco	*òsohbuhkoh*	sliced leg of veal
palliard	*pahyahr*	veal filet
petto	*petoh*	breast

Pasta as a dessert: noodles with figs

piccata	peekahtah	veal medallions
piede	pyehdeh	foot
polmone	pòlmohneh	lungs
rognoni	rònyohnee	kidneys
scaloppa	skahlòpah	scallop (of pork, veal)
spezzatino	spetsahteenoh	veal stew
testa	testah	head
trippa	tripah	tripe
zampone	dzahmpohneh	stuffed pigs' feet

Poultry

anitra	ahneetrah	duck
galletto	gahletoh	chicken
oca	òkah	goose
tacchino	tahkeenoh	turkey

Before the eyes of the public at a sidewalk café: street artists in Rome

Wild Game

camoscio	*kahmohshoh*	chamois
capriolo	*kahpreeyòloh*	venison
cervo	*chehrvoh*	red deer
cinghiale	*cheengyahleh*	wild boar
faggiano	*fahjahnoh*	pheasant
faraona	*fahrahohnah*	guinea hen
lepre	*lehpreh*	hare
pernice	*pehrneecheh*	partridge
piccione	*pichohneh*	dove
tordo	*tohrdoh*	thrush

Sauces

salsa al burro	*sahlsah ahl bùroh*	butter sauce
salsa alle noci	*sahlsah ahleh nòchee*	sauce made from ground nuts and cream
salsa bolognese	*sahlsah bòlònyehzeh*	tomato sauce with meat
salsa napoletana	*sahlsah nahpohleh-tahnah*	simple tomato sauce
salsa verde	*sahlsah vehrdeh*	parsley sauce with oil egg, spices and capers
pesto alla genovese	*pestoh ahlah jehnovehzeh*	green basil sauce with pine nuts, parmesan cheese and garlic

Side Dishes/Vegetables

l'asparago	*lahspahrahgoh*	asparagus
le carote	*leh kahrohteh*	carrots
il cavolfiore	*il kahvohlfyohreh*	cauliflower
i cavolini di Bruxelles	*ee kahvohleenee dee bruksel*	Brussels sprouts
il cavolo	*il kahvohloh*	cabbage
le cipolle	*leh cheepohleh*	onions
la fava	*lah fahvah*	beans
i funghi	*ee fungee*	mushrooms
le olive	*leh ohleeveh*	olives
le patate	*leh pahtahteh*	potatoes
le paste	*leh pahsteh*	noodles/pasta
il pepe	*il pehpeh*	green pepper

i piselli	*ee peezelee*	peas
i pomodori	*ee pomohdoree*	tomatoes
il porro	*il poroh*	leeks
il riso	*il reezoh*	rice
lo spinacio	*loh spinahchoh*	spinach

Desserts

budino	*buhdeenoh*	pudding
cassata	*kahsahtah*	icecream dessert
gelato	*jehlahtoh*	icecream
macedonia	*mahchehdohnyah*	fruit salad
panettone	*pahnetohneh*	cake
torta	*tortah*	pastry
zabaglione	*dzahbahlyohneh*	a frothy dessert made with egg yolk, sugar and Marsala wine

Cheeses

Bel Paese	*bel pahehzeh*	soft, creamy cheese
Brancolino	*brahnkohleenoh*	goat cheese
Gorgonzola	*gorgòndzohlah*	blue cheese
Mozzarella	*mòtsahrelah*	mozzarella cheese
Parmigiano	*pahrmeejahnoh*	parmesan cheese
Provolone	*prohvohlohneh*	piquant cheese
Pecorino	*pehkoreenoh*	sheep's cheese
Ricotta	*reekòtah*	ricotta cheese
Romano	*rohmahnoh*	sheep' s cheese
Stracchino	*strahkeenoh*	a soft cheese

In Italy, coffee is not simply coffee

the small, black and strong coffee known as "espresso" is called *caffè* in Italy. However, there are also a number of other variations on the coffee bean in Italy: *caffé lungo* is less strong and is served in larger cups *caffé ristretto* is somewhat stronger *caffé macchiato* (= speckled) is served with a few drops of milk (the opposite being *latte macchiato* which is milk served with a relatively small amount of coffee). *Caffé corretto* is improved with the addition of some alcohol like grappa, brandy or amaro. *Caffé freddo* is served chilled cappuccino or *cappuccio* is *caffè* with steamed milk. The name comes from the brown colour of the hoods worn by the Capucin monks.

Shopping

The stores in Italy are open on weekdays from 9 am to 7:30 pm, interrupted by a long lunch break from 1 to 4 pm. Depending on the season and the region, there is half a day during the week where the stores remain closed. This is often Monday morning.

| business hours | le ore d'apertura | *lohreh dahpehrtuhrah* |
| open/closed | aperto/chiuso | *ahpehrtoh/kyuhzoh* |

Types of Stores

antique shop	le antichità	*le ahnteekeet<u>ah</u>*
bakery	il fornaio	*il fornahyoh*
(secondhand) book store	la libreria (antiquaria)	*lah librehreeyah (ahnteekw<u>a</u>hreeyah)*
butcher shop	il macellaio	*il machelahyoh*
camera store	il negozio di articoli fotografici	*il nehgohtsyoh dee ahr<u>tee</u>kohlee fohtohgrahfeechee*
children's wear	l'abbigliamento per bambini	*lahbeelyahmentoh pehr bahmbeenee*
dairy shop	la latteria	*lah lahtereeyah*
department store	il grande magazzino	*il grahndeh mahgahtseenoh*
drugstore	la drogheria	*lah drohgehreeyah*
electrical goods store	negozio di articoli eletrici	*il nehgohtsyoh dee ahr<u>tee</u>kohlee elehtreechee*
vegetable/fruit stand	l'erbivendolo/il fruttivendolo	*lehrbeevendohloh/il fruteevendohloh*
groceries	gli alimentari	*lyee ahleementahree*
hairdresser/barber	il parruchiere	*il pahrukyehreh*
hardware/ironmonger	il negozio di ferramenta	*il nehgohtsyoh dee feramentah*
household goods	gli articoli casalinghi	lyee ahrteekohlee kahzalingee
jeweller	la gioielleria	*lah joyelehreeyah*

ladies' wear/men's wear	l'abbigliamento per donne/uomini	*lahbeelyahmentoh pehr dòneh/wohmeenee*
leather goods	la pelletteria	*lah peletehreeyah*
newsstand	il giornalaio	*il johrnahlahyoh*
optician	l'ottico	*lòteekoh*
pharmacy	la farmacia	*lah fahrmahcheeyah*
seafood/fish shop	la pescheria	*lah peskehreeyah*
second hand store	il rigattiere	*il reegahtyehreh*
shoe store	il negozio di calzature	*il nehgohtsyoh dee kahltsahtuhreh*
sporting goods store	il negozio di gli articoli sportivi	*il nehgohtsyoh dee lyee ahrteekohlee sporteevee*
stationery shop	la cartoleria	*lah kahrtohlehreeyah*
tailor	la sartoria	*lah zahrtoreeah*
tobacco shop	la tabaccheria	*lah tahbahkehreeyah*

Campo di Fiori: the flower market in Rome

toy store	il negozio di giocattoli	*il nehgohtsyoh dee jyòkahtohlee*
watchmaker	l'orologiaio	*lorohlohjahyoh*
wine shop	il negozio di vini	*il nehgohtsyoh dee veenee*

In the Shops and at the Market

May I help you?	Desidera?	*dehzeedehrah?*
I am just looking, thank you.	Sto solo guardando, grazie.	*stoh sohloh gwahrdahn-doh, grahtsyë*
Could you give me one kilo/pound of ...	Mi dia per favore un chilo/un mezzo chilo di ...	*mee deeyah pehr fah-voreh uhn keeloh/uhn metsoh keeloh dee ...*
How much does that cost?	Quanto costa questo?	*kwahntoh kòstah kwestoh?*
small/large/less/more	piccolo/grande di meno/di più	*peekohloh/grahndeh dee mehnoh/dee pyuh*
May I give you more?	Può essere un po'di più?	*pwoh esehreh uhn poh dee pyuh?*
Anything else?	Altro?	*ahltroh?*
That is all, thank you.	Basta così, grazie.	*bahstah kòzee, grahtsyë*
bag	il sacchetto	*il sahketoh*
bunch	il mazzo	*il mahtsoh*
can	la lattina	*la lahteenah*
shopping bag	la borsa/il sacchetto	*lah borzah/il sahketoh*
package	il pacco/pacchetto	*il pahkoh/pahketoh*
slice	la fetta	*lah fetah*

At the Post Office

stamps for a letter/ a postcard to the US/ Great Britain	francobolli per una lettera/cartolina per Inglaterra/America	*frahnkohbòlee pehr uhnah leterah/kahrtoh-leenah pehre inglah-terah/ahnmehreekah*
I would like to send a (small) package to ...	Vorrei spedire un (pacchetto) pacco per ...	*vorehee spehdeereh uhn (pahketoh) pahkoh pehr ...*
How do I have to stamp this letter?	Con quanto devo francare questa lettera?	*kòn kwahntoh dehvoh frahnkahreh kwestah leterah*

| I would like to pick up a letter. | Vorrei ritirare una spedizione. | *vorehee reeteerahreh uhnah spedeetsyohneh* |
| general delivery | fermo posta | *fehrmoh pòstah* |

Vocabulary Post Office

air mail	la posta aerea	*lah pòstah ahehrehah*
express letter	un espresso	*uhnehspresoh*
letter	la lettera	*lah leterah*
mailbox	la cassetta postale/ la buca delle lettere	*la kahsetah pòstahleh/ lah buhkah deleh letereh*
post office	l'ufficio postale	*lufeechoh pòstahleh*
postal money order	il modulo di versamento	*il mòduhloh dee versahmentoh*
postcard	la cartolina (illustrata)	*lah kartohleena (iluhstrahtah)*
registered letter	una raccomandata	*unah rahkohmahn-dahtah*
wire of money	il vaglia telegrafico	*il valyah telehgrah-feekoh*

Department Stores and Supermarkets

Where can I find ... ?	Dove si trova?	*dòveh see trohvah?*
colour	la colore	*lah kohloreh*
size	la grande	*lah grahndeh*
material/cloth	la stoffa	*lah stòfah*
basement	il sottosuolo	*il sòtohswohloh*
bedding department	il reparto letti	*il rehpahrto letee*
candy	i prodotti dolciari	*ee pròdòtee dòlchahree*
cashier	la cassa	*lah kahsah*
complaint	il reclamo	*il rehklahmoh*
dry goods/haberdashery	le mercerie	*leh mehrchehreeyë*
elevator	l'ascensore	*lahshensohreh*
escalator	la scala mobile	*lah skahlah mohbeeleh*
first/second/third/ fourth floor	primo/secondo/terzo/ quatro piano	*preemoh/sehkòndoh/ tehrtsoh/kwahtroh pyahnoh*
gifts	gli articoli da regalo	*lyee ahrteekohlee dah rehgahloh*

groceries	gli alimentari	*lyee ahleementahree*
leather goods	le pelletterie	*leh peletereeyë*
parking garage	il parcheggio a più piani	*il pahrkehjoh ah pyuh pyahnee*
sales clerk	il commesso (masc.) la commessa (fem.)	*il komesoh/ lah komesah*
sporting goods	gli articoli sportivi	*lyee ahrteekohlee sporteevee*
toys	i giocattoli	*ee johkahtohlee*

Vocabulary: Foods — Fruits, Vegetables and Spices

almonds	le mandorle	*leh mahndorleh*
anise	l'anice	*lahneecheh*
apple	la mela	*leh mehlah*
apricot	le albicocche	*leh albeekòkeh*
artichoke	il carciofo	*il kahrchohfoh*
asparagus	l'asparago	*lahspahrahgoh*
banana	la banana	*lah bahnahnah*
basil	il basilico	*il bahzeeleekoh*
bay leaf	la foglia d'alloro	*la fòlyah dahloroh*
beans	la fava	*lah fahvah*
(red) beets	la barbabietola rossa	*lah bahrbahbyehtohla ròsah*
bell pepper	il peperone	*il peperohneh*
cabbage	il cavolo	*il kahvohloh*
capers	i capperi	*ee kahpehree*
carrots	le carote	*leh kahrohteh*
cauliflower	il cavolfiore	*il kahvohlfyohreh*
celery	il sedano	*il sehdahnoh*
cherries	le cigliege	*leh cheelyehjeh*
chervil	il cerfoglio	*il cherfohlyoh*
chestnuts	le castagne	*leh kahstahnyë*
chickory	la cicoria di Bruxelles	*la cheekoreeah dee bruksel*
chickpeas	i ceci	*ee chehchee*
cocoa	il cacao	*il kahkow*
coconut	la noce di coco	*la nohche dee kohkoh*

cucumber	il cetriolo	*il chehtreeyohloh*
currants	i ribes	*ee reebehs*
dates	i datteri	*ee dahtehree*
dill	l'aneto	*lahnehtoh*
eggplant/aubergine	la melanzana	*lah mehlahndzahnah*
fennel	il finocchio	*il feenòkyoh*
figs	i fichi	*ee feekee*
fruit	la frutta	*lah frutah*
garlic	l'aglio	*lahlyoh*
grapefruit	il pompelmo	*il pompehlmoh*
grapes	l'uva	*luhvah*
hazel nuts	le nocciole	*leh nòchohleh*
head lettuce	la lattuga	*lah lahtuhgah*
hot peppers	peperoncini	*pehpehrohncheenee*
honeydew melon	il melone	*il mehlohneh*
leeks	il porro	*il pòroh*

The market at the Milvio Bridge in Rome

lemon	il limone	_il leemohneh_
lentils	le lenticchie	_leh lenteekyeh_
maiz/corn	il mais	_il mahyeez_
marjoram	la maggiorana	_lah mahjorahnah_
mint	la menta	_lah mehntah_
mustard	il senape	_il sehnahpeh_
nutmeg	la noce moscata	_lah nohcheh mòskahtah_
nuts	le noci	_leh nohchee_
olives	le olive	_le ohleeveh_
onions	le cipolle	_le chipòleh_
orange	l'arancia	_lahrahnchah_
oregano	l'origano	_loreegahnoh_
parsley	il prezzemolo	_il pretsemohloh_
peach	la pesca	_lah peskah_
peanuts	le noccioline americane	_leh nòchyohleeneh ahmehreekahneh_
pear	la pera	_lah pehrah_
peas	i piselli	_ee peezelee_
pepper	il pepe	_il pehpeh_
pickles	i cetrioli sott'aceto	_ee chehtreeyohlee sòtahchehtoh_
pineapple	l'ananas	_lahnahnahs_
plum	la prugna	_la pruhnyah_
potatoes	le patate	_leh pahtahteh_
pumpkin	la zucca	_lah dzukah_
quince	la cotogna	_lah kohtohnyah_
radish	il rafano	_il rahfahnoh_
raisins	l'uva secca	_luhvah sehkah_
raspberries	i lamponi	_ee lahmpohnee_
rice	il riso	_il reezoh_
rolled oats	fiocchi d'avena	_fyòkee dahvehnah_
rosemary	il rosmarino	_il rohzmahreenoh_
saffron	lo zafferano	_loh dzahfehrahnoh_
sage	la salvia	_lah zahlvyah_
salt	il sale	_il sahleh_
spinach	lo spinacio	_lo speenahchoh_

strawberries	le fragole	*leh frahgohleh*
string beans/runner beans	il fagiolo	*il fahjohloh*
tarragon	l'estragone	*lehstrahgohneh*
thyme	il timo	*il teemoh*
tomatoes	i pomodori	*ee pòmohdohree*
vegetables	le verdure	*leh vehrduhreh*
walnuts	la noce	*lah nohcheh*
watermelon	il cocomero	*il kòkohmehroh*

Other Foods

baby food	l'alimentazione infantile	*lahleementahtsyohneh infahnteeleh*
beef	il manzo	*il mahndzoh*
beer	la birra	*lah beerah*
bread	il pane	*il pahneh*
butter	il burro	*il buroh*
cake	il dolce	*il dòlcheh*
candy/sweets	i dolci	*ee dòlchee*
cheese	il formaggio	*il formahjoh*
chicken	il galletto/il pollo	*il gahletoh/il pòloh*
chocolate	la cioccolata	*lah chòkohlahtah*
coffee	il caffè	*il kahfeh*
cold cuts/sausage	la salsiccia	*lah sahlseechah*
cookies/biscuits	i biscotti	*ee beeskòtee*
eggs	l'uovo (s.)/le uova (pl.)	*lwohvoh/leh wohvah*
escargots/snails	le lumache	*leh luhmahkeh*
fish	il pesce	*il pesheh*
flour	la farina	*lahfahreenah*
ground meat/ minced meat	la carne macinata	*lah kahrneh macheenahtah*
lamb/mutton	l'agnello	*lahnyeloh*
lemonade/soft drink	la limonata	*lah leemohnahtah*
mayonnaise	la maionese	*lah mahyohnehzeh*
meat	la carne	*lah kahrneh*
milk	il latte	*il lahteh*
pork	il maiale	*il mahyahleh*
rabbit	il coniglio	*il koneelyoh*

(hard) rolls	i panini	*ee pahneenee*
salad oil	l'olio	*lohlyoh*
sausages/hotdogs	le salsiccette	*leh sahlseecheteh*
seafood	i frutti di mare	*ee frutee dee mahreh*
sour cream	la panna da cucina	*lah pahnah dah kuhcheenah*
sugar	lo zucchero	*loh dzukehroh*
tea	il tè	*il teh*
turkey	la tacchina	*lah tahkeenah*
veal	il vitello	*il veeteloh*
vinegar	l'aceto	*lahchehtoh*
whipping cream	la panna dolce	*lah pahnah dòlcheh*
wine	il vino	*il veenoh*
yogurt	il iogurt	*il yohguhrt*

Other Expressions

deep fried	fritto	*fritoh*
dried	secco/essicato	*sekoh/eseekahtoh*
for grilling/boiling/frying/roasting	per la griglia/per bollire/per arrostire	*pehr lah gril/ pehr bòleerah/pehr arohsteereh*
fresh	frescho	*freskoh*
ground/minced	macinato	*mahcheenahtoh*
moldy	ammuffito	*ahmuhfeetoh*
raw	crudo	*kruhdoh*
rotten	guasto	*gwahstoh*
sliced	tagliato a fette	*talyahtoh ah feteh*

Vocabulary: Clothing

bathing cap	la cuffia da bagno	*lah kufyah dah bahnyoh*
bathing suit/swimsuit	il costume da bagno	*il kòstuhmeh dah bahnyoh*
bathing trunks	i calzoncini da bagno	*ee kahldzohncheenee dah bahnyoh*
bathrobe	l'accappatoio	*lahkahpahtoyoh*
bikini	il costume da bagno a due pezzi/bikini	*il kòstuhmeh dah bahnyoh ah duheh petsee/beekeenee*
blazer	il blazer	*il blehzer*

blouse	la camicetta/la blusa	*la kahmeechetah/ lah bluhzah*
boots	gli stivali	*lyee steevahlee*
bra	il reggiseno	*il rejeesehnoh*
cap/hat	il berretto/il cappello	*il beretoh/il kahpeloh*
coat	il cappotto	*il kahpòtoh*
cotton	il cotone	*il kòtohneh*
dress	il vestito	*il vesteetoh*
galoshes/wellingtons	gli stivali di gomma	*lyee steevahlee dah gòmah*
gloves	i guanti	*ee gwahntee*
handkerchief	il fazzoletto	*il fahtsohletoh*
jacket	la giacca	*lah jahkah*
jeans	i jeans	*ee jeenz*
leather	la pelle	*lah peleh*
nightgown/nightshirt	la camicia da notte	*lah kahmeechah dah nòteh*
pyjamas	il pigiama	*il peejahmah*
rain jacket/coat	l'impermeabile	*limpehrmehahbeeleh*
sandals	i sandali	*ee sahndahlee*
scarf	il fazzoletto/ la sciarpa (da collo)	*il fahtsohletoh/lah schahrpah (dah kòloh)*
scarf (winter)	il foulard	*il fuhlahr*
shirt	la camicia	*lah kahmeechah*
shoes	le scarpe	*leh skahrpeh*
shorts	gli shorts	*lyee shorts*
skirt	la gonna	*lah gònah*
socks	i calzini	*ee kahltseenee*
stockings	le calze	*leh kahltseh*
suit (women's)/(men's)	il tailleur/il àbito	*il tayër/il ahbeetoh*
sun hat	il cappello da sole	*il kahpeloh dah sohleh*
sweater/jumper	il maglia/il pullover	*il mahlyah/il pulohvehr*
tie	la cravatta	*lah krahvahtah*
tights/panty hose	il collant	*il kòlah*
trousers/slacks	i pantaloni	*ee pahntahlohnee*
t-shirt	il T-shirt	*il tee-shërt*
underpants	le mutande	*leh muhtahndeh*

undershirt	la maglietta	*lah mahlyehtah*
underwear	la blanchera intima	*la blahnkerah inteemah*
vest	il panciotto/il gilè	*il panchòtoh/il jeel<u>eh</u>*
wool	la lana	*lah lahnah*

---

i **Different countries — different sizes**

Women must be careful when looking for shoes in Italy since sizes are different from those in other continental European countries. The continental size 38 (British: 5; American 6) is size 44 in Italy. Strangely enough, this is only true for women's shoes; men's sizes are the same.

Other Articles

aftershave	la lozione da barba	*lah lòtsyohneh dah bahrbah*
alarm clock	la sveglia	*lah svehlyah*
battery	la pila	*la peelah*
books	i libri	*ee leebree*
bottle opener	l'apribottiglie	*lahpreebòt<u>ee</u>lyë*
button	il bottone	*il bòt<u>oh</u>hneh*
can opener	l'apriscatole	*lahpreeskahtohleh*
charcoal	il carbone da grill	*il kahrbohneh dah gril*
cigar	il sigaro	*il s<u>ee</u>gahroh*
cigarettes	le sigarette	*leh seegahreteh*
cigarillo	il sigaretto	*il seegahretoh*
cleanser/scouring powder	l'abrasivo	*lahbrahseevoh*
comb	il pettine	*il peteeneh*
condoms	i preservativi	*ee prehzervahteevee*
corkscrew	il cavatappi	*il kahvahtahpee*
dish cloth	lo straccio per lavare i piatti	*loh strahchoh pehr lahvahreh ee pyahtee*
dish washing liquid	il deterviso (per le stoviglie)	*il dehterveezoh (pehr leh stohveelyeh)*
deodorant	il deodorante	*il dehohdorahnteh*
dustbin liners/ garbage bags	il sacchetto delle immondizie	*il sahchetoh deleh imohndeetsyë*
elastic	l'elastico	*lehlahsteekoh*
electric shaver	il rasoio	*il rahzoyoh*

flashlight/torch	la torcia	*lah torchah*
hairbrush	la spazzola per i capelli	*lah spahtsohlah* *pehr ee kahpelee*
laundry detergent	il detersivo	*il dehterzeevoh*
light bulb	la lampadina	*lah lahmpahdeenah*
lighter	l'accendino	*lahchendeenoh*
magazine	il periodico/la rivista	*il pereeyohdeekoh/lah* *reevistah*
matches	i fiammiferi	*ee fyahmm<u>ee</u>fehree*
mirror	lo specchio	*loh spekyoh*
nail file	la limetta da unghie	*lah leemetah dah ungee*
nappies/diapers	i pannolini	*ee pahnohleenee*
(sewing) needle	l'ago (per cucire)	*lahgoh (pehr kucheereh)*
newspaper	il giornale	*il jornahleh*
powder	la cipria	*lah ch<u>ee</u>preeyah*
razor blades	le lame	*leh lahmeh*
safety pin	la spilla da sicurezza	*lah spilah dah* *seekuhrehtsah*
sanitary napkins	gli assorbenti	*lyee ahsorbehntee*
scissors	le forbici	*leh forbeechee*
shampoo	lo shampoo	*loh shahmpuh*
shaving soap/cream	il sapone/la crema da barba	*il sahpohneh/lah* *krehmah dah babah*
shoelaces	il laccio per scarpio	*il lachoh per skahrpyoh*
soap	il sapone	*il sahpohneh*
stationery	la carta da lettere	*lah kahrtah dah letereh*
sun glasses	gli occhiali da sole	*lyee òkyalee dah sohleh*
suntan lotion	l'olio solare	*l<u>o</u>hyoh sohlahreh*
tampons	il tampone	*il tahmpohneh*
thread	il filo per cucire	*il feeloh pehr kucheereh*
tobacco	il tabacco	*il tahbahkoh*
toilet paper	la carta igienica	*lah kahrtah ijehneekah*
toothbrush	lo spazzolino da denti	*loh spahtsohleenoh* *dah dentee*
toothpaste	il dentifricio	*il denteefreechoh*
umbrella	l'ombrello	*lombrehloh*
watch	l'orologio	*lorohlohjoh*

Sightseeing

Italy remains heavily influenced by the Roman Catholic Church even today. When visiting churches, one should therefore note the following: shoulders and knees must be covered. Despite the hot climate, women should always have a scarf handy to cover the shoulders and both men and women should forgo wearing shorts.

What to see?

I am looking for the tourist information office.	Cerco l'ufficio informazioni (l'ente del turistico).	*Cherkoh luhfeetchoh informahtsyohnee (lenteh del tuhreesteekoh)*
Where can I find the tourist office?	Dove si trova l'ente del turismo?	*dòveh see trohvah lenteh del tuhreezmoh?*
Do you have a map of the city?	Ha una pianta della città?	*ah uhnah pyahntah delah cheetah?*
Is this brochure also available in English?	Esiste anche in inglese questo dépliant?	*ehzeesteh ahnkeh in inglehzeh kwestoh dehpleeah?*
What is worth seeing here?	Che cosa si può visitare in città?	*keh kòsah see pwoh vizeetahreh in cheetah?*
When is the museum open?	Quando è aperto il museo?	*kwahndoh eh ahpehrtoh il muhzehyoh?*
How much is admission?	Quanto costa l'ingresso?	*kwahntoh kòstah lingresoh?*
I would like to buy a catalogue/a ticket for the exhibition.	Vorrei un catalogo/un biglietto d'ingresso per la mostra.	*vorehee uhn kahtahlohgoh/uhn beelyetoh dingresoh pehr lah mòstrah*
Is there a charge for parking?	E un parcheggio a pagamento?	*eh uhn pahrkejoh ah pahgahmentoh?*
Is there any discount for students/children?	C'è una riduzione per scolari/studenti/bambini?	*cheh uhnah reedutsyohneh pehr skohlahree/stuhdentee/bahmbeenee?*

Do you have an international student ID?	Ha una tessera di studenti?	*ah uhnah tesehrah dee stuhdentee?*
Is there a sightseeing tour/a guided tour through the city?	Ci sono giri turistici organizzate della città/visite guidate della città?	*chee sohnoh jiree tuh-reesteechee orgahnee-dzahteh delah cheetah/ viseetahteh gweedahteh delah cheetah?*
Where does the tour start?	Dove si parte per il giro della città?	*dòveh see pahrteh pehr il jeeroh delah cheetah?*
Are there also guided tours in English?	Ci sono anche visite guidate in inglese?	*chee sohnoh ahnkeh viseeteh gweedahteh in inglehzeh?*

Vocabulary: Culture

abbey	l'abbazia	*lahbahtseeyah*
alleyway	il vincolo	*il veenkohloh*
altar	l'altare	*lahltahreh*

A side trip to Venice — simply a must for every visitor to Italy

amber	l'ambra	lahmbrah
annex	l'edificio annesso	lehdeefeechoh ahnesoh
antiquity	l'antichità	lahnteekeetah
arch	il arco	il ahrkoh
Art Nouveau	lo stilo floreale/il liberty	loh steeloh florehahleh/il leebehrtee
avenue	il viale alberato	il vyahleh ahlbehrahtoh
baroque	il barocco	il bahròkoh
base	il piedistallo	il pyehdeestahloh
basilica	la basilica	lah bahzeeleekah
brick	il mattone	il mahtohneh
bridge	il ponte	il pònteh
bronze	il bronzo	il brònzoh
building	l'edificio	lehdeefeechoh
capital	il capitello	il kahpeeteloh
castle	il castello	il kahsteloh
castle	la fortezza	lah fortetsah
cemetery	il cimitero	il cheemeetehroh
century	il secolo	il sehkohloh
ceramic	la ceramica	lah cherahmeekah
chapel	la capella	lah kahpelah
choir	il coro	il koroh
church	la chiesa	lah kyehza
city	la città	la cheetah
classicism	il classicismo	il klahseecheezmoh
clay	l'argilla	lahrjilah
cloister	il chiostro	il kyohstroh
columns	le colonne	leh kohlòneh
cross	la croce	lah krohcheh
crypt	la cripta	lah kreeptah
dome	la cupola	lah kuhpohlah
engraving	l'incisione su rame	lincheezyohneh suh rahmeh
excavations	gli scavi	lyee skahvee
exhibition	la mostra	lah mòstrah
factory	la fabbrica	lah fahbreekah

furniture	i mobili	_ee mohbeelee_
gallery (art)	la galeria	_lah gahlehreeyah_
gallery (architectural)	il matroneo	_il mahtrohnehoh_
garden	il giardino	_il jahrdeenoh_
gargoyle	il doccione	_il dòchyohneh_
gate, city gate	il portone	_il portohneh_
glass	il vetro	_il vehtroh_
Gothic	il gotico	_il gohteekoh_
half-timber	il traliccio	_il trahleechoh_
ivory	l'avorio	_lahvoreeyoh_
library	la biblioteca	_lah beebleeyohtehkah_
manor house	la villa (signorile)	_lah vilah (seenyoreeleh)_
marble	il marmo	_il mahrmoh_
marketplace	il mercato	_il mehrkahtoh_
Middle Ages	il medioevo	_il mehdyohehvoh_
modern period	l'età moderna	_lehtah mohdehrnah_
mosaik	il mosaico	_il mohsahyeekoh_
mosque	la moschea	_lah mòskehyah_
museum	il museo	_il muhzehyoh_
nave	la navata	_lah nahvahtah_
painting	il quadro/il dipinto	_il kwahdroh/_ _il deepeentoh_
pillar	il pilastro	_il peelahstroh_
porcelain	la porcellana	_lah porchelahnah_
portal	il portale	_il portahleh_
Renaissance	il rinascimento	_il rinahsheementoh_
Romanesque	il romanico	_il rohmahneekoh_
Romans	i romani	_ee rohmahnee_
Romantic	il romanticismo	_il rohmahntee-_ _cheezmoh_
roof	il tetto	_il tetoh_
ruins	la rovina	_lah rohveenah_
sarcophagus	il sarcofago	_il sahrkohfahgoh_
school	la scuola	_lah skwohlah_
sculptures	le sculture	_leh skultuhreh_
sill	la cornice	_lah korneecheh_

slate	l'ardesia	*lahrdehzyah*
square/plaza	la piazza	*lah pyahtsah*
statue	la statua	*lah stahtuhah*
synagogue	la sinagoga	*lah seenahgohgah*
temple	il tempio	*il tempyoh*
theater	il teatro	*il tehahtroh*
tower	il torre	*il toreh*
town (city) hall	il municipo	*il muhneecheepoh*
vessel	il recipiente	*il rehcheepyehnteh*
village	il villaggio	*il vilahjoh*
wall	il muro	*il muhroh*
window	la finestra	*lah feenehstrah*
wood	il legno	*il lehnyoh*

Vocabulary: Nature and Geography

aquarium	l'acquario	*lahkwahreeyoh*
bay	la baia	*lah bahyah*
beach	la spiaggia	*la spyahjah*
bird sanctuary	il parco di protezione degli uccelli	*il pahrkoh dee prohteh-tsyohneh delyee uchelee*
botanical gardens	l'orto botanico	*lortoh bohtahneekoh*
canal	il canale	*il kahnahleh*
ravine/canyon	il precipizio	*il prehcheepeetsyoh*
cave	la grotta	*lah gròtah*
cavern	la caverna	*la kahvehrnah*
cliff paintings	le iscrizioni rupestri	*leh eeskritsyohnee ruhpehstree*
climate	il clima	*il kleemah*
desert	il deserto	*il dehsehrtoh*
dune	la duna	*lah duhnah*
English garden	il giardino all'inglese	*il jahrdeenoh alinglehzeh*
estuary/mouth	la foce	*la fohche*
forest	il bosco	*il bòskoh*
forest (large)	la foresta	*lah forehstah*
gravel	la ghiaia	*lah gyayah*

hill	il colle	*il kòleh*
lagoon	la laguna	*lah lahguhnah*
lake	il lago	*il lahgoh*
landscape	il paesaggio	*il pahyehzahjoh*
lava	la lava	*la lahvah*
meadow	il prato	*il prahtoh*
Mediterranean	il Mediterraneo	*il mehdeetehrahnehyoh*
mountain	il monte	*il mònteh*
mountain masif	il massiccio	*il mahsichoh*
mountain range	le montagne	*leh mòntahnyeh*
mudflats	il bassofondo	*il bahsohfòndoh*
nature reserve	il parco nazionale	*il pahrkoh nahtsyohnahleh*
sceenic overlook	il belvedere	*il belvehdehreh*
observatory	l'osservatorio	*òsehrvahtoreeyoh*
panorama	il panorama	*il pahnohrahmah*

A view of the Colosseum and Titus Arch: Roman history comes to life

promontory	lo spuntone	*loh spuntohneh*
quicksand	la sabbia mobile	*lah sahbyah mohbeeleh*
rapids	la caraterra	*lah kahrahtehrah*
reeds	la canna palustra/ le canne	*lah kahnah pahluhstrah/ leh kahneh*
reservoir	il lago artificiale	*il lahgoh ahrteefee-chahleh*
river	il fiume	*il fyuhmeh*
rock	la roccia	*lah ròchah*
sand	la sabbia	*lah sahbyah*
sand bank	il banco di sabbia	*il bahnkoh dee sahbyah*
sea/ocean	il mare	*il mahreh*
sound	il sund	*il sund*
spring (water)	la sorgente	*lah sorjenteh*
strait/sound	lo stretto	*loh stretoh*
stream	il ruscello	*il ruhsheloh*
valley	la valle	*lah vahleh*
vinyards	i vignetti	*ee vinyetee*
volcano	il vulcano	*il vuhlkahnoh*
waterfall	la cascata	*lah kahskahtah*
zoo	lo zoo	*loh dzoh*

Vocabulary: Flora and Fauna

alder	l'ontano	*lòntahnoh*
animals	gli animali	*lyee ahneemahlee*
ash	il frassino	*il frahseenoh*
beech	il faggio	*il fahjoh*
birch	la betulla	*lah behtulah*
birds	gli uccelli	*lyee uchelee*
bird of prey	l'uccello rapace	*lucheloh rahpahcheh*
bush	l'arbusto	*lahrbuhstoh*
bushes/underbrush	la boscalglia	*lah bòskahlyah*
chestnut	il castagno	*il kahstahnyoh*
cypress	il cipresso	*il cheepresoh*
deer	i cervi	*ee chehrvee*
dove/pigeon	il piggione	*il peejohneh*

duck	l'anatra	_lahnahtrah_
elm	l'olmo	_lohlmoh_
fir	l'abete rosso	_lahbehteh ròsoh_
frog	la rana	_lah rahnah_
goose	l'oca	_lòkah_
horse-chestnut	l'ippocastano	_lipohkahstahnoh_
insects/bugs	gli insetti	_lyee insetee_
jellyfish	la medusa	_lah mehduhzah_
lizard	la lucertola	_lah luhchehrtohlah_
maple	l'acero	_lahchehroh_
mosquito	la zanzara	_lah dzahndzahrah_
mussel	la conchiglia	_lah kònkeelyah_
oak	la quercia	_lah kwehrchah_
palm tree	la palma	_lah pahlmah_
pine	il pino	_il peenoh_
plane tree	il platano	_il plahtahnoh_
plants	le piantare	_leh pyahntahreh_
poplar	il pioppo	_il pyòpoh_
quail	ka quaglia	_lah kwahlyah_
scorpion	lo scorpione	_loh skorpyohneh_
Scotch pine	il pino silvestre	_il peenoh silvehstreh_
seagull	il gabbiano	_il gahbyahnoh_
sea urchin	il riccio di mare	_il richoh dee mahreh_
snail	la lumacha	_lah luhm<u>ah</u>kah_
snake	il serpente	_il sehrpenteh_
spruce	l'abete rosso	_lahbehteh ròsoh_
toad	il rospo	_il ròspoh_
tree	l'albero	_lahlbehroh_
turtle	la tartaruga	_lah tahrtahruhgah_
viper	la vipera	_lah veepehrah_
weeping willow	il salice piagente	_il sahleecheh pyahjehnteh_
wild boar	il cinghiale	_il cheengyahleh_
willow	il salice	_il s<u>ah</u>leecheh_

Sports, Recreation and Entertainment

On the following pages, you will find the most important phrases for an evening of entertainment at the theatre, the discotheque or at a *birrerìa* (pub) as well as phrases relating to all types of sports and recreation.

Theatre, Cinema and Concert

English	Italian	Pronunciation
What is playing tonight at the theater/cinema?	Che cosa c'è al teatro/al cinema stasera?	keh còsah cheh ahl tehahtroh/ahl cheenehmah stahsehrah?
When does the performance/the concert/the film begin?	Quando comincia la rappresentazione/lo spettacolo/il concerto/il film?	kwahndoh kohmeencha lah rahprehzentahtsyohneh/loh spetahkohloh/il kònchehrtoh/il film?
How long does the ... last?	Quanto tempo dura ...?	kwahntoh tehmpoh duhrah ...?
Where can I get tickets?	Dove posso comprare i biglietti?	dòveh pòsoh kòmprahreh ee beelyetee?
advance ticket office/at the door	il botteghino/la cassa	il bòtehgeenoh/lah kahsah
I would like two tickets for this evening/tomorrow ...	Un biglietto/due biglietti per stasera/domani ...	uhn beelyetoh/duheh beelyetee pehr stahsehrah/dohmahnee ...

Vocabulary: Theatre

English	Italian	Pronunciation
box	il palco	il pahlkoh
circle	la galleria	lah gahlehreeyah
cloakroom	il guardaroba	il gwahrdahrohbah
first/second balcony	il matroneo primo/secondo	il mahtrohnehoh preemoh sehkòndoh
parquet	le prime file della platea	leh primeh feeleh delah plahtehah

row	la fila	*la feelah*
seat	il posto	*il pòstoh*
usher	la maschera	*lah mahskehrah*

Discotheques, Dancing and Pubs

Where is a good disco/nightclub/bar around here?	Dove si trova una buona discoteca/un buon locale noturno/un buon bar?	*dòveh see trohvah uhnah bwohnah diskohtehkah/uhn bwohn lohkahleh nòtuhrnoh/ uhn bwohn bahr?*
We would like to go dancing.	Vorremmo andare a ballare.	*voremoh ahndahreh ah bahlahreh*
How long are you open?	Fino a che ora è aperto il locale?	*feenoh ah keh orah eh ahpehrtoh il lohkahleh?*
Are the drinks expensive?	Sono care le bevande?	*sohnoh kahreh leh behvahndeh?*

Almost as if petrified by exertion: gargoyles at the Pantheon Fountain

What type of people go there?	Che pubblico c'è in quel locale?	*keh publeekoh cheh in kwel lohkahleh?*
tourists/local people	i turisti/i locali	*ee tuhreestee/ee lohkahlee*
What kind of music?	Quale musica?	*kwahleh muhzeekah?*
May I bring you home?	Posso accompagnar-La?	*pòsoh akòmpahnyahr-lah?*
Will we see each other again?	Ci rivediamo?	*chee reevehdyahmoh?*
Leave me alone!	Mi lasci in pace!	*mee lashee in pahcheh!*

Sports and Recreation

Fishing

| Where is there good fishing around here? | Dove si può pescare con l'amo qui vicino? | *dòveh see pwoh pes-kahreh kòn lahmoh kwee veecheenoh?* |
| valid for one day/month | valido per un giorno/un mese | *vahleedoh pehr uhn jornoh/uhn mehzeh* |

Vocabulary: Fishing

annual permit	la tessera annua	*lah tesehrah ahnnuhah*
bait	il verme da pesca	*il vehrmeh dah peskah*
carp	la carpa	*lah kahrpah*
cod	il merluzzo comune	*il merlutsoh kòmuhneh*
deep-sea fishing	la pesca d'altro mare	*lah peskah dahltroh mahreh*
fishing	pescare con l'amo	*peskahreh kòn lahmoh*
fishing license	la tessera di pesca	*lah tesehrah dee peskah*
fishing line	la lenza	*lah lentsah*
fishing rod	la canna da pesca	*lah kanah dah peskah*
lake	il lago	*il lahgoh*
perch	il pesche persico	*il pescheh pehrseekoh*
pike	il luccio	*il luchoh*
pond	lo stagno	*loh stahnyoh*
river	il fiume	*il fyuhmeh*
rowboat	la barca a remi	*lah bahrkah ah rehmee*

salmon	il salmone	_il sahlmohneh_
sea	il mare	_il mahreh_
spinner/spoon	il cucchiaino	_il kukyaheenoh_
stream	il ruscello	_il ruhsheloh_
trout	la trota	_lah trohtah_
weights	il piombo	_il pyòmboh_

Golf

| golf club | la mazza da golf | _lah mahtsah dah gòlf_ |
| golf course | il golf | _il gòlf_ |

Tennis

tennis court	il campo da tennis	_il kahmpoh dah tenis_
tennis racket	la racchetta (da tennis)	_lah rahchehtah (dah tenis)_
How much does one hour cost?	Quanto costa un'ora?	_kwahntoh kòstah uhnorah?_
one-hour lesson	un'ora di lezione	_uhnorah dee lehtsyohneh_

Aquatic Sports

Where can I rent ...?	Dove si possono noleggiare ...?	_dòveh see pòsonoh nohlehjahreh ...?_
surfboards/equipment	tavole per il surf/ l'equipaggiamento	_tahvohleh pehr il surf/ lehkweepajahmentoh_
scuba diving equipment	l'attrezzeatura da subacqueo	_lahtretsahtuhrah dah subahkwehyoh_
a sailboat	una barca da vela	_uhnah bahrkah dah vehlah_
What does the boat cost per hour?	Quanto costa all'ora la barca?	_kwahntoh kòstah ahlohrah lah bahrkah?_
Is the beach sandy/ stony/rocky?	La spiaggia è sabbiosa/pietrosa/ scogliosa?	_lah spyahjah eh sah-byohsah/pyehtrohsah/ skohlyohzah?_
Is the beach patrolled?	C'è un custode della spiaggia/un bagnino di salvataggio?	_cheh uhn kustohdeh delah spyahjah/uhn bahnjeenoh dee sahlvahtahjoh?_

Is the beach suitable for children?	E anche adatta per bambini?	*eh ahnkeh ahdahtah pehr bahmbeenee?*
Is the water clean?	L'acqua è pulita?	*lahkwah eh puhleetah?*
Are there any jellyfish?	Ci sono meduse?	*chee sohnoh mehduhzeh?*
When is low tide/ high tide?	Quando c'è la bassa/ l'alta marea	*kwahndoh cheh lah bahsah/lahltah mahrehyah?*

Vocabulary: Aquatic Sports

canoe	la canoa	*lah kahnohwah*
indoor/outdoor swimming pool	la piscina coperta/all'aperto	*lah peesheenah koh-pehrtah/ahlahpehrtoh*
sailing	navigare a vela	*nahveegahreh ah vehlah*

After a strenuous climb to the top, time for a break: hikers in Abruzzi

scuba diving	practicare l'immersione/sommozzare	*prakteekahre limehrzyohneh/sòmohtsahreh*
shower	la doccia	*lah dòchah*
snorkel	il tubo respiratorio	*il tuhboh dee rehspee rahtoreeyoh*
swimming/bathing	nuotare	*nwohtahreh*
surfing	praticare il surfing/fare il surf	*prahkteekahreh il surfing/fahreh il surf*
water-skiing	lo sci acquatico	*loh skee ahkwahteekoh*

Horseback Riding / Cycling

| Is there a riding stable nearby? | C'è una scuderia qui vicino? | *chèh uhnah skuhdehreeyah kwee veecheenoh?* |
| Where can I rent a horse? | Dove posso noleggiare un cavallo? | *dòveh pòsoh nohlehjahreh uhn kahvahloh?* |

Those who enjoy horseback riding will find an opportunity to do this in Italy

I would like to go horseback riding.	Vorrei fare una passegiata a cavallo.	*vorehee fahreh uhnah pahsehjahtah ah kahvahloh*
How much does it cost per hour?	Quanto costa un'ora di equitazione?	*kwahntoh kòstah uhnorah ehkweetah-tsyohneh?*
I would like to rent a bicycle.	Vorrei noleggiare una bicicletta?	*vorehee nohlehjahreh uhnah beecheekletah?*
How much does it cost per hour/per day?	Quanto costa all'ora/al giorno?	*kwahntoh kòstah ahlor-ah/ahl jornoh?*
A deposit is required.	Bisogna lasciare una cauzione.	*beezònyah lashahreh uhnah kowtsyohneh*
How much is the deposit?	A quanto ammonta la cauzione?	*ah kwahntoh ahmòntah lah kowtsyohneh?*
Does the bicycle have more than one gear?	Ha più velocità la bicicletta?	*ah pyuh vehlohcheetah lah beecheekletah?*

Vocabulary: Horseback Riding/Cycling

basket	il cestino della bicicletta	*il chehsteenoh delah beecheekletah*
child's seat	il sedile per bambini	*il sehdeeleh pehr bahmbeenee*
lady's bicycle	la bicicletta per donne	*lah beecheekletah pehr dònah*
men's bicycle	la bicicletta per uomini	*lah beecheekletah pehr wohmeenee*
mountain bike	la mountainbike	*lah mowntenbi:k*
pedal brake	il freno a contrapedale	*il frehnoh ah kòtrahpehdahleh*
three-speed bicycle	la bicicletta a tre velocità	*lah beecheekletah ah treh vehlohcheetah*

Winter Sports

beginner	principianti	*preencheepyahntee*
binding	gli attacchi	*lyee ahtahkee*
chairlift	la seggiovia	*lah sejohveeyah*
cross-country skiing	lo sci di fondo	*loh skee dee fòndoh*

cross-country course	la pista di fondo	*lah peestah dee fòndoh*
downhill skiing	lo sci in discesa	*loh skee dee deeshehzah*
ice skating	il pattinaggio su ghiaccio	*il pahteenahjoh suh gyahchoh*
ski instructor	il maestro/la maestra di sci	*il mahyehstroh/lah mahyehstrah dee skee*
ski lift	lo ski-lift	*loh skee-lift*
ski suit	la tenuta da sci	*lah tehnuhtah dah skee*
ski wax	la sciolina	*lah shohleenah*
skis	gli sci	*lyee skee*
skiing lessons	il corso di sci	*il korsoh dee skee*
sledding	andare in slitta	*ahndahreh in zlitah*
slope	la pista	*lah peestah*

Other Sports

bowling	il gioco dei birilli	*il jòkoh dehee beerilee*
basketball	la pallacanestro	*lah pahlahkahnehstroh*
canoeing	lo sport della canoa	*loh sport delah kahnohah*
football (soccer)	il calcio	*il kahlchoh*
gliding	il volare a vela	*il vohlahreh ah vehlah*
hang-gliding	il deltaplano	*il deltahplahnoh*
hiking	il camminare	*il kahmeenahreh*
hunting	la caccia	*lah kahchah*
miniature golf	il minigolf	*il meeneegòlf*
motor sport	il motorismo	*il mohtoreezmoh*
mountain climbing	l'alpinismo	*lahlpeeneezmoh*
parachuting	il paracadutismo	*il pahrahkahduh-teezmoh*
ping-pong	il tennis da tavolo	*il tenis dah tahvohloh*
rafting	la canoa	*lah kahnohwah*
sauna	la sauna	*lah sownah*
volleyball	la pallavolo	*lah pahlahvohloh*

Services

On the following pages are a number of phrases and terms which will prove helpful in situations ranging from having one~s hair cut to having film developed and one's camera repaired.

At the Hair Dresser's

How much is a haircut?	Quanto costa il taglio dei capelli?	*kwahntoh kòstah il tahl-yoh dehyee kahpelee?*
I would like to have my hair cut.	Mi tagli i capelli, per favore.	*mee tahlyee ee kah-pelee, pehr fahvoreh*
about that short/long	Corti cosi/lunghi cosi	*kortee koh<u>zee</u>/lungee koh<u>zee</u>*
A shave, please.	Mi faccia la barba, per favore.	*mee fahcha lah bahr-bah, pehr fahvoreh*

Vocabulary: Hair Dresser

beard	la barba	*lah bahrbah*
blow-dry	asciugare con l'asciugacapelli	*ashuhgahreh kòn lahshuhgahkahpelee*
curlers	i bigodini	*ee beegohdeenee*
dandruff	la forfora	*lah forforah*
fringe/bangs	il pony	*il pohnee*
full beard	la barba piena	*lah bahrbah pyehnah*
hair dryer	il casco l'asciugacapelli	*il kahskoh lahshuhgahkahpelee*
hair dyeing/tinting	colorare/tingere i capelli	*kohlorahreh/tinjehreh ee kahpelee*
hair treatment	il trattamento per i capelli	*il trahtahmentoh pehr ee kahpelee*

in the back/in the front	di dietro/sul davanti	*dee dyehtroh/ sul dahvahntee*
layered cut	il taglio a gradini	*ee tahlyoh ah grahdeenee*
moustache	i baffi	*ee bahfee*
perm(anent)	la permanente	*leh pehrmahnenteh*
shampoo	la shampoo	*lah shahmpuh*
sideburns	le basette	*leh bahzeteh*
toupet	il toupet	*il tuhpeh*
washing	il lavare	*il lahvahreh*
wig	la parrucca	*lah pahrukah*

Cosmetics

eyebrows	le sopracciglie	*leh sohprahcheelyeh*
facial	la maschera	*leh mahskehrah*
make-up	truccare	*trukahreh*
manicure	il manicure	*il mahneekuhreh*
massage	il massaggio	*il mahsahjoh*
pedicure	il pedicure	*il pehdeekuhreh*
solarium	il banco abbronzante	*il bahnkoh ahbrohdsahnteh*

Repairs

Optician

My glasses are broken.	I miei occhiali si sono rotti.	*ee myehee òkyahlee see sohnoh ròtee*
frames	la montatura degli occhiali	*lah mòntahtuhrah dehlye òkyahlee*
lenses	le lenti	*leh lentee*
Can you repair the frame?	Può riparare la montatura?	*pwoh reepahrahreh lah mòntahtuhrah?*
Can you put the lenses into a new frame?	Può mettere le lenti in nuova montatura?	*pwoh metehreh leh lentee in nwohvah mòntahtuhrah?*
How long will it take to repair?	Quanto duretà la riparazione?	*kwahntoh duhrehtah lah reepahrahtsyohneh?*

soft/hard contact lenses	le lenti a contatto morbide/dure	*leh lentee ah kòntahtoh morbeedeh/duhreh*
cleaning solution	la soluzione sterilizzante	*lah sohlutsyohneh stehreeledzahnteh*
soaking solution	la soluzione per la conservazione	*lah sohluhtsyohneh pehr lah kònsehrvah-tsyohneh*

Tailor

Can you sew in a new zipper?	Mi può cucire una nuova chiusura lampo?	*mee pwoh kuhcheereh uhnah kyuhzuhrah lahmpoh?*
The lining is torn.	La fòdera si è staccata.	*lah fohdehrah see eh stahkahtah*
Can you mend this?	Mi può rammendare questo?	*mee pwoh rahmehn-dahreh kwestoh?*

Vocabulary: Tailor

button hole	l'occhiello	*lòkyeloh*
buttons	il bottone	*il bòtohneh*
collar	il colletto	*il kòletoh*
elastic band	l'elastico	*lehlahsteekoh*
hem	l'orlo	*lorloh*
lining	la fòdera	*lah fohdehrah*
material	la stoffa	*lah stòfah*
pocket	la tasca	*lah tahskah*
sleeve	la manica	*lahmahneekah*
zipper	la chiusura lampo	*lah kyuhzuhra lahmpoh*

Laundry/Cleaners'

dryer	l'essiccatrice	*lesikahtreecheh*
ironing	stirare	*steerahreh*
laundromat	la lavanderia	*lah lahvahndehreeyah*
laundry detergent	il detersivo	*il dehtehrseevoh*

normal wash cycle	il lavaggio	*il lahvahjoh*
pre-wash cycle	il prelavaggio	*il prehlahvahjoh*
remove the stain	togliere una macchia	*tolyehreh uhnah mahkyah*
washing machine	la lavatrice	*lah lahvahtreecheh*
to wash	lavare	*lahvahreh*

Shoe Repair

Could you re-sole these shoes?	Mi può risolare queste scarpe?	*mee pwoh reesohlahreh kwesteh skahrpeh?*
My shoes need new heels.	Ho bisogno di nuovi tacchi.	*oh beezònyoh dee nwohvee tahkee*
This shoe needs to be stretched.	Bisogna allargare questa scarpa.	*beezònyoh ahlahgahreh kwestah skahrpah*
Do you also have shoe polish?	Ha anche lucido per scarpe?	*ah ahnkeh luhcheedoh pehr skahrpeh?*
When can I pick up the shoes?	Quando posso venire a prendere le scarpe?	*kwahndoh pòsoh veh-neereh ahl prendereh leh skahrpeh?*

Vocabulary: Shoe Repair

boots	gli stivali	*lyee steevahlee*
heel	il tacco	*il tahkoh*
sandals	i sandali	*ee sahndahlee*
shoelaces	il laccio per scarpe	*il lahchoh pehr skahrpeh*
shoes	le scarpe	*leh skahrpeh*
sole	la suola	*lah swohlah*

Film Developing and Camera Repairs

| I would like to have this film developed. | Vorrei fore sviluppare questa pellicola. | *vorehee fohreh sveelu-pahreh kwestah pelee-kohlah* |
| Black and white/color prints of each negative. | Di ogni foto una copia in blanco e nero/colori. | *dee ònyee fohtoh uhnah kòpyah in byahnkoh eh nehroh/ah kohloree* |

How much does the developing/ do the prints cost?	Quanto costa lo sviluppo/quanto costano le copie?	*kwahntoh kòstah loh sveelupoh/kwahntoh kòstahnoh leh kòpyeh?*
Can you make an enlargement?	Me ne può fare un ingradimento?	*meh neh pwoh fahreh uhningrahdeementoh?*
The film is overexposed/ underexposed.	La pellicola è sovra-esposta/sottoesposta.	*lah peleecohlah eh sohvrahrehspòstah/ sòtohehspòstah*
The film is not advancing.	La pellicola non è trasportata.	*lah peleekohlah nohn eh trahnsportahtah*
Can you repair the camera?	Mi può riparare la macchina fotografica?	*mee pwoh reepahrahreh lah mahkeenah fohtoh-grahfeekah?*

Vocaulary: Photography

battery	la pila	*lah peelah*
black and white film	la pellicola in blanco e nero	*lah peleekohlah in byahnkoh ee nehroh*
color print film	la pellicola in colori	*lah peleekohlah in kohloree*
film cartridge	la pellicolla a cassetta	*lah peleekohlah ah kahsetah*
film speed	la sensibiltà della pellicola	*lah senseebeeleetah delah peleekohlah*
flash	il flash	*il flash*
lens	l'obiettivo	*lòbyeteevoh*
light meter	l'esposimetro	*lespohzeemehtroh*
roll film	il rullino	*il ruhleenoh*
shutter release	lo scatto	*loh skahtoh*
slide film	la pellicola per diapositivi	*lah peleekohlah pehr deeyah pohzeeteevee*
35 mm film	la pellicola per fotografie di formato piccolo	*lah peleekohlah pehr fohtohgrahfeeyeh dee formahtoh peekohloh*

Health Care

In case it is necessary to visit a doctor during one's stay in Italy, one should definitely check into various travel health insurance plans. Costs for treatment must be paid immediately, making a detailled invoice necessary for reimbursement. In some regions, tourists are also treated by the Medical Emergency Service (*pronto soccorso*).

Finding a Doctor

Where can I find a doctor?	Dove si trova un mèdico?	*dòveh see trohvah uhn mehdeekoh?*
Where is the nearest hospital/doctor's office?	Dov'è il prossimo ospedale/ambulatorio mèdico?	*dòveh il pròseemoh òspehdahleh/ambulah-toreeyoh mehdeekoh?*

Vocabulary: Health Care
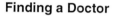

dentist	il dentista	*il dehnteestah*
dermatologist	il dermatologo	*il dehrmahtohlohgoh*
doctor/general practitioner	il mèdico	*il mehdeekoh*
ear, nose and throat specialist	l'otorinolaringoiatra	*lohtohreenohlah reengoyahtrah*
eye doctor	l'oculista	*lòkuhleestah*
gynaecologist	il ginecologo	*il jeenehkohlohgoh*
hospital	l'ospedale	*lòspehdahleh*
international health insurance form	il modulo per una cura medica internazionale	*il mòduhloh uhnah kuhrah mehdeekah intehrnahtsyohnahleh*
orthopedic surgeon	l'ortopedico	*lortohpehdeekoh*
pediatrician	il pediatra	*il pehdeeyahtrah*
pharmacy	la farmacia	*lah fahrmahcheeyah*
prescription	la prescrizione	*lah prehskreetsyohneh*
surgeon	il chirugo	*il keeruhrgoh*
treatment room	lo studio mèdico	*loh stuhdeeyoh mehdeekoh*
waiting room	l'anticamera	*lahnteekahmehrah*

Where is the problem?

How can I help you?	Come posso aiutarLa?	*kòmeh pòsoh ayuhtahrlah?*
I'm ill.	Sono malato/-a.	*sohnoh mahlahtoh/-ah*
I have pains	Ho dolori.	*oh dohloree*
I am injured	sono ferito/-a.	*sohnoh fehreetoh/-ah*
I injured myself.	Mi sono ferito/-a.	*mee sohnoh fehreetoh/ fahreetah.*
I fell.	Sono caduto/-a.	*sohnoh kahduhtoh/-ah*
I was bitten.	Sono stato/-a morso/-a.	*sohnoh stahtoh/-ah morsoh/-ah*
snake/dog/ cat/mouse/rat	il serpente/il cane/il gatto/il toppo/il ratto	*il sehrpehteh/il kahneh/il gahtoh/il tòpoh/il rahtoh*
I was stung by a ...	Sono stato/-a punto/a per ...	*sohnoh stahtoh/-ah puntoh/-ah pehr ...*
bee/wasp fly/mosquito/ scorpion/ jellyfish/ sea urchin	l'ape/la vespa/ la moscha/la zanzara/lo scorpione/ la medusa il riccio di mare	*lahpeh/lah vespah/ lah mòskah/lahdzahn zhahrah/loh skorpyoh-neh/lah mehduhzah/ il reechoh dee mahreh*
I have a cold.	Ho preso un raffreddore.	*oh prehzoh uhn rahfredohreh*
I have a cough.	Ho la tosse.	*oh lah tòseh*
Could you prescribe something for ...?	Mi può prescrivere qualcosa contro ...?	*mee pwoh prehskree-vereh kwahlkohzah kòntroh ...?*
I feel nauseous/dizzy.	Mi sento male/ho il capogrio.	*mee sentoh mahleh/oh il kahpojeeroh.*

Symptoms

Where is the problem?	Dove Le fa male?	*dohveh leh fah mahleh?*
I have ...	Ho..	*oh ...*
aching joints	i dolori articolari	*ee dohloree ahrtee-kohlahree*
backache	i dolori alla schiena	*ee dohloree ahlah skyehnah*
bleeding/hemorrhage	l'emorragia	*lemorahjah*

breathing difficulties	difficoltà di respiro	*difeekohltah dee rehspeeroh*
bruise	l'ematoma	*lehmahtohmah*
cold	il raffreddore	*il rahfredohreh*
constipation	la costipazione	*lah kòsteepahtsyohneh*
contusion/bruise	la contusione	*lahkòntuhzyohneh*
cough	la tosse	*lah tòseh*
cramp (in the calf)	il crampo (del polpacio)	*il krahmpoh (del pohlpahchoh)*
diarrhea	la diarrea	*lah deeyahrehyah*
fever	la febbre	*lah febreh*
food allergy	l'allergia da alimenti	*lahlehrjah dah ahleemehntee*
hay fever	la febbre da fieno	*lah febreh dah fyehnoh*
headache	il mal di testa	*il mahl dee tehstah*
mentrual pain	i dolori degli organi genitili femminili.	*ee dohloree delyee jehneeteelee femeeneelee.*
nausea	il giramento di stomaco	*il jeerahmentoh dee stohmahkoh*
ringing in the ears	il ronzio auricolare	*il rontsyoh owreekohlahreh*
sore throat	il mal di gola	*il mahl dee gohlah*
stomach ache	il mal di vente	*il mahl dee vehnteh*
sweating	la traspirazione	*lah trahspeerahtsyohneh*
the chills	i brividi di febbre	*ee breeveedee dee febreh*
toothache	il mal di denti	*il mahl dee dehntee*
vomiting	il vomito	*il vohmeetoh*
wound/cut	la ferita	*lah fehreetah*

Where does it hurt?

abdomen	il ventre	*il vehntreh*
ankle	il malleolo	*il mahlehohloh*
appendix	l'appendice	*lahpehndeecheh*
arm	il braccio (sing.)/ le braccia (pl.)	*il brahchoh/ leh brahchah*

back	la schiena	*lah skyehnah*
bladder	la vescica	*lah vesheekah*
bone	l'osso (sing.)/	*lòsoh/*
	le ossa (pl.)	*leh òsah*
bronchial tubes	i bronchi	*ee brònkee*
calf	il polpaccio	*il polpahchoh*
chest	il petto	*il petoh*
ear	l'orecchio	*lorekyoh*
elbow	il gomito	*il gohmeetoh*
esophagus	l'esofago	*lehzohfahgoh*
eye	l'occhio	*lòkyoh*
eyelid	la palpebra	*lah pahlpehbrah*
finger	il dito (sing.)/	*il deetoh/*
	le dita (pl.)	*leh deetah*
foot	il piede	*il pyehdeh*
hand	la mano (sing.)/	*lah mahnoh/*
	le mani (pl.)	*leh mahnee*
heart	il cuore	*il kwohreh*
intestine	l'intestino	*lintehsteenoh*
kidney	il rene	*il rehneh*
knee	il ginocchio	*il jeenòkyoh*
lung	il polmone	*il polmohneh*
nail	l'unghia	*lungyah*
nerves	i nervi	*ee nehrvee*
nose	il naso	*il nahzoh*
rib	la costola	*lah kòstohlah*
skin	la pelle	*lah peleh*
stomach	lo stomaco	*loh stohmahkoh*
throat	la gola	*lah gohlah*
thumb	il pollice	*il pòleecheh*
toes	il dito del piede	*il deetoh del pyehdeh*
tongue	la lingua	*la linguah*
tooth	il dente	*il denteh*
I am allergic/	Sono allergico/	*sohnoh ahlehrjeekoh*
diabetic.	diabetico.	*deeyahbehteekoh*
I am pregnant	Sono incinta.	*sohnoh incheentah*

I wear contact lenses/ dentures.	Porto lenti di contatto/ una protesi dentaria.	*portoh lehntee dee kòntahtoh/uhnah prohtehzee dentahreeyah*
I have a pacemaker.	Porto uno stimolatore cardiaco.	*portoh uhnoh steemohlahtoreh kahrdeeyahkoh*
I am allergic to certain foods: ...	Soffro di un'allergia alimentare per ...	*sòfroh dee uhnahlehrjeeyah aleementahreh pehr ...*

Illnesses and Ailments

AIDS	l'AIDS	*lah-eedz*
bladder infection	la cistite	*lah cheesteeteh*
blister	la bolla	*lah bòlah*
broken arm/leg	la frattura del braccio/della gambe	*lah frahtuhrah del brahchoh/delah gahmbeh*
bronchitis	la bronchite	*lah brònkeeteh*
burn	la scottatura	*lah skòtahtuhrah*
chickenpox	la varicella	*lah vahrechelah*
concussion	la commozione cerebrale	*lah kòmohtsyohneh chehrehbrahleh*
corn	il callo	*il kahloh*
flu	l'influenza	*linfluhehntsah*
food poisoning	l'intossicazione da alimenti	*lintòseekahtsyohneh dah aleementee*
German measles	la rosolia	*lah rohzohleeyah*
haemmorrhoids	le emorrodi	*leh ehmohroheedee*
hay fever	la febbre da fieno	*lah febreh dah fyehnoh*
heat stroke	il colpo di calore	*il kohlpoh dee kahlohreh*
jaundice	l'itterizia	*litehreetsyah*
malaria	la malaria	*lah mahlahreeyah*
measles	il morbillo	*il morbilyoh*
middle ear infection	l'otite media	*lòteeteh mehdyah*
migraine	l'emicrania	*lehmeekrahneeyah*
mumps	la parotite	*lah pahrohteeteh*
mycosis	l'infezione micosa	*linfehtsyohneh meekohsah*
nose bleed	l'emorragia nasale	*lehmorahjah nahzahleh*

period, menstruation	le mestruazioni	*le mehstruhahtsyohnee*
pulled tendon	lo stiramento del tendine	*lo steerahmentoh del tehndeeneh*
rash	l'etruzione cutanea	*lehtrutsyohneh kuhtahnehyah*
salmonella poisoning	l'avvelenamento di salmonelle	*lahvelehnahmentoh dee sahlmohnehleh*
sciatica	l'ischialgia	*liskeeyahljah*
sprain	la slogatura	*lah slohgahtuhrah*
sunburn	la scottatura solare	*lah skòtahtuhrah sohlahreh*
sunstroke	l'insolazione	*linsohlahtsyohneh*
tetanus	il tetano	*il tehtahnoh*
tonsilitis	la tonsillite	*lah tònseeleeteh*
torn ligament	lo strappo	*loh strahpoh*
torn muscle	lo strappo muscolare	*loh strahpoh muskohlahreh*

First Aid and Medications

bandage	la fascia/la benda	*lah fahshah/lah behndah*
capsule	la capsula	*lah kahpsuhlah*
cast	l'ingessatura	*linjesahtuhrah*
compress	la compressa	*lah kòmpresah*
cough medicine/syrup	il rimedio/sciroppo contro la tosse	*il reemehdyoh/shee-ròpoh kòntroh lah tòseh*
dressing	la fasciatura	*lah fashahtuhrah*
drops	le gocce	*le gòcheh*
help	l'aiuto	*layuhtoh*
ointment	la pomata	*lah pohmahtah*
pain reliever	il calmante	*il kahlmahnteh*
pills	le compresse	*leh kòmpreseh*
plaster/band-aid	il cerotto	*il cheròtoh*
sleeping pills	il sonnifero	*il sòneefehroh*
thermometer	il termometro	*il tehrmohmehtroh*

Glossary

English — Italian

A

abbey – *l'abbazia*
abdomen – *il ventre*
above – *sopra*
accellorator pedal – *il pedale dell'acceleratore*
aching joints – *i dolori articolari*
adhesive tape – *il nastro adesivo*
adults – *gli adulti*
after – *dopo*
afternoon – *il pomeriggio*
aftershave – *la lozione de barba*
against – *contro*
age – *l'età*
air conditioning – *l'aria condzionata*
air pressure gauge – *il misuratore della pressione dell'aria*
airport – *l'aeroporto*
alarm clock – *la sveglia*
alder – *l'ontano*
All Saints' Day – *l'Ognissanti*
alleyway – *il vincolo*
almonds – *le mandorle*
also – *anche*
altar – *l'altare*
amber – *l'ambra*
anchovies – *le acciuge*
and – *e*
angleiron – *il gomito*
animals – *gli animali*
anis – *l'anice*
ankle – *la malleolo*

annex (of a building) – *l'edificio annesso*
annual pass – *la tessera annua*
antiques – *le antichità*
antiquity – *l'antichità*
apartment – *l'appartamento*
appendix – *l'appendice*
apple – *la mela*
apricots – *le albicocche*
April – *aprile*
aquarium – *l'acquario*
aqueduct – *l'acquaedotto*
area code – *il prefisso telefonico*
arm – *il braccio (sing.)/ le braccia (pl.)*
arrival – *l'arrivo*
arrival time – *l'ora d'arrivo*
Art Nouveau – *il liberty, lo stile floreale*
artichoke – *il carciofo*
ash tree – *il frassino*
asparagus – *l'asparago*
at night – *di notte*
attention – *attenzione*
aubergine – *la melanzana*
August – *agosto*
autumn, fall – *l'autunno*
axle – *l'asse*
axle bearing – *l'asse di supporto*

B

baby food – *l'alimentazione infantile*
back – *la schiena*
backache – *i dolori alla schiena*

bag – *la busta/il sacchetto/la tascha*
bait – *il verme da pesca*
baker – *il fornaio*
balcony – *il balcone/(theatre) il matroneo*
ball bearing – *il cuscinetto a sfere*
banana – *la banana*
bandage – *la benda, la fascia, la fasciatura*
band-aid – *il cerotto*
bangs – *il pony*
bank – *il banco*
baptismal font – *il fonte battesimale*
barber – *il barbiere*
baroque – *il barocco*
basil – *il basilico*
basilica – *la basilica*
basketball – *la pallacanestro*
bathing cap – *la cuffia de bagno*
bathing shoes – *le scarpe de bagno*
bathrobe – *l'accappatoio*
bathroom – *il bagno*
battery (small) – *la pila*
battery (car) – *la batteria*
bay – *la baia*
beach – *la spiaggia*
beams – *il contrafforte*
beans – *la fava*
beard – *la barba*
because – *perchè*
bed – *il letto*
beech tree – *il faggio*
beef – *il manzo*
beer – *la birra*

beginner/advanced – _principianti/non principianti_

behind – _dietro_

beige – _beige_

bell – _il campanello/(large) la campana_

bell pepper – _il peperone_

between – _tra_

beverages – _la bevande_

bicycle basket – _il cestino della bicicletta_

bicycle seat – _la sella_

bicycle stand – _il posteggio_

bike path – _la pista ciclabile_

bikini – _il costume de bagno a due pezzi (bikini)_

bill – _il conto_

birch – _la betulla_

bird of prey – _l'uccello rapace_

bird sanctuary – _il parco di protezione degli uccelli_

birds – _gli uccelli_

biscuits – _i biscotti_

black – _nero_

bladder – _la vescica_

bladder infection – _la cistite_

blanket – _la coperta_

blazer – _il blazer_

blister – _la bolla_

blouse – _la blusa, la camicetta_

blow drying – _asciugare con l'asiugacapelli_

blue – _blu, azzurro_

body (of car) – _la carrozzeria_

boiled – _bollito_

bone(s) – _l'osso (sing.)/le ossa (pl.)_

bonnet (car) – _il cofano_

book – _il libro_

booking – _la prenotazione, la registrazione_

bookstore, bookseller – _la libreria_

boot (car) – _il portabagagli_

boot/trunk lid – _il coperchio del portabagagli_

boots – _gli stivali_

botanical garden – _l'orto botanico_

bottle opener – _l'apribottiglie_

bottom bracket bearing – _il supporto dei pedali_

boulevard – _la viale alberato_

box (theatre) – _il palco_

bra – _il reggiseno_

brake fluid – _l'olio per freni_

brake lining – _la guarnizione del freno_

brake pedal – _il pedale del freno_

brake shoe – _il pattino del freno_

Brazil nut – _la noce del Pará_

bread – _il pane_

bread rolls – _i panini_

breaded – _impanato_

breakfast – _la prima colazione_

breathing difficulties – _difficoltà di respiro_

brick – _il coccio, il mattone_

bridge – _il ponte_

broccoli – _broccoli_

bronchial tubes – _i bronchi_

bronchitis – _la bronchite_

bronze – _il bronzo_

brook – _il ruscello_

brown – _marrone, (skin, hair) – scuro_

bruise – _la contusione_

brush – _il pennello_

Brussels sprouts – _i cavolini di Bruxelles_

building – _l'edificio_

bumper – _il paraurti_

bunch – _il mazzo_

burn – _la scottatura_

bus – _l'autobus_

bus stop – _la fermata_

bush, shrub – _l'arbusto_

bush – _il cespuglio_

busy – _occupato_

but – _ma, però_

butcher – _il macellaio_

butter – _il burro_

button – _il bottone_

buttonhole – _l'occhiello_

buzzing in the ears – _il ronzio auricolare_

bypass – _la strada di raccordo_

C

cabbage – _il cavolo_

cable – _il cavo_

calf (leg) – _il polpaccio_

calliper brake – *il freno sul cerchione*

camera – *la macchina fotografica*

camera shop – *il negozio di articoli fotografici*

camper – *la roulotte*

camping area – *il camping/il campeggio*

camping permit – *la tessera di campeggio*

camshaft – *l'albero a camme*

can – *la lattina*

can opener – *l'apriscatole*

canal – *il canal*

candy – *i dolci*

cane – *la canna palustre*

canister – *la tanica*

canoeing – *la canoa*

canoeing – *lo sport della canoa*

canyon – *il precipizio*

cap – *il berretto*

capers – *i capperi*

capital (of column) – *il capitello*

capsule – *la capsula*

car – *la macchina*

car door – *lo sportello d'auto*

car horn – *il clacson*

car radio – *l'auotradio*

car rental agency – *l'agenzia di noleggio di automobili*

car sleeper train – *il treno navetta*

car (motion) sickness – *il mal d'auto*

caravan, camping vehicle, RV – *l'autocaravan*

caravan – *la roulotte*

carburettor – *il carburatore*

Carnival – *il carnevale*

carp – *la carpa*

carriage number (train) – *il numero della carrozza*

carrier (bicycle) – *il portabagagli*

carrots – *le carote*

carwash – *impianto di autolavaggio*

castle – *il castello*

catalytic converter – *la marmitta catalitica*

cauliflower – *il cavolfiore*

caution – *attenzione*

caution train – *attenzione al treno*

cave – *la grotta*

cave with stalactites and stalagmites – *la grotta con stalattiti e stalagmiti*

cavern – *la caverna*

cellery – *il sedano*

cemetery – *il cimitero*

centimetre – *il centimetro*

central telephone switchboard – *la centrale telefonica*

century – *il secolo*

ceramics – *la ceramica*

chain – *la cantena*

chain grease – *il grasso per la catena*

chairlift – *la seggiovia*

chambermaid – *la cameriera*

chapel – *la capella*

charcoal – *il carbone de grill*

chasis – *il carrello*

cheese – *il formaggio*

cherries – *le cigliege*

chervil – *il cerfoglio*

chest – *il petto*

chestnuts – *le castagne*

chicken – *il pollo, il galletto*

chickenpox – *la varicella*

chickory – *la cicoria di Bruxelles*

chickpeas – *i ceci*

children – *i bambini*

children's clothing – *l'abbigliamento per bambini*

child's bed – *il letto per bambini*

child's seat – *il sedile per bambini*

chisel – *lo scalpello*

chives – *l'erba cipolina*

chocolate – *la cioccolata*

choir – *il coro*

Christmas – *Natale*

church – *la chiesa*

church tower – *il campanile*

cigar – *il sigaro*

cigarette lighter – *l'accendino*

cigarettes – *le sigarette*

cigarillo – *il sigaretto*

circle (theatre) – *la galleria*

city – *la città*

city hall – *il municipio*

classicism – *il classicismo*

clay – *l'argilla*

cleaning solution (contact lenses) – *la soluzione sterilizzante*

clenser – *l'abrasivo*

cliff paintings – *le iscrizioni rupestri*

climate – *il clima*

cloakroom – *il guardaroba*

cloister – *il chiostro*

clutch (pedal) – *(il pedale della frizione*

coat – *il cappotto*

coconut – *la noce di coco*

cod – *il merluzzo comune*

coffee – *il caffé*

cold – *freddo*

cold (illness) – *il raffreddore*

collar – *il colletto*

collect call – *la telefonata R*

coloured – *a colori*

colourful – *colorato*

columns – *le colonne*

comb – *il pettine*

compact car – *l'utilitaria*

compartment (train) – *lo scompartimento*

comprehensive insurance – *l'assicurazione con copertura totale*

compress – *la compressa*

concussion – *la commozione cerebrale*

condoms – *i preservativi*

confectionery – *la pasticceria*

connecting flight – *il volo di coincidenza*

constipation – *la costipazione*

construction work – *lavori in corso*

construction zone – *cantiere*

contact lenses – *le lenti a contatto*

contusion – *la contusione*

cooker – *il fornello*

cookies – *i biscotti*

cooking area – *il posto per cucinare*

coolant hose – *il conduttore dell'acqua del radiatore*

cooler grille – *la griglia del radiatore*

corkscrew – *il cavatappi*

corn – *il mais*

corn (on foot) – *il callo*

Corpus Christi – *Corpus Domini*

corridor – *il corridoio*

cotton – *il cotone*

cotton wool – *l'ovatta*

couchette car – *la carrozza con cucccete*

cough – *la tosse*

cough remedy – *il rimedio contro la tosse*

cough syrup – *lo sciroppo contro la tosse*

country code – *il prefisso nazionale*

cow – *la vacca*

cover (charge) – *il coperto*

cramp – *il crampo*

crankshaft – *l'albero a gomiti*

crazy golf – *il minigolf*

crockery – *i piatti*

cross – *la croce*

crossroads – *il quadrato*

cross-country bus – *l'autobus interurbano*

cross-country skiing – *lo sci di fondo*

cross-country trail – *la pista di fondo*

cross-point screwdriver – *il cacciavite a croce*

crowbar – il gomito

crypt – *la cripta*

cucumber – *il cetriolo*

currants – *i ribes*

curve – *la curva*

customs – *la dogana*

cutlery – *le posate*

cycling – *il ciclismo*

cyclist – *il ciclista*

cypress – *il cipresso*

D

dairy shop – *la latteria*

damage – *il danno*

dancing – *ballare*

dandruff – *la forfora*

danger – *il pericolo*

dark – *scuro*

dashboard – *il pannello portastrumenti*

date – *la data*

date of birth – *la data di nascita*

date of entry/departure
 – la data di entrata/di
 uscita

date of issue – la data
 di emissione

dates – i datteri

day after tomorrow –
 dopo domani

December – dicembre

deep-sea fishing – la
 pesca d'alto mare

deer – cervi

delay – il ritardo

delicatessen – il nego-
 zio di specialitá ga-
 stronomiche

dentist – il dentista

deodorant – il deodo-
 rante

department store – il
 grande magazzino

departure – la partenza

departure gate – l'im-
 barco

departure time – l'ora
 di partenza

deposit – la cauzione

dermatologist – il der-
 matologo

desert – il deserto

dessert – il dessert, il
 dolce

detour – deviazione

deversion – deviazione

diapers – i pannolini

diarrhoea – la diarrea

diesel – gasolio

dill – l'aneto

dimmer switch – il com-
 mutatore delle luci

direct train – il treno diretto

dish brush – la spazzo-
 la per le stoviglie

dish cloth – lo straccio
 per lavare i piatti

dish washing liquid – il
 detersivo per le sto-
 viglie

dishes – i piatti

do not overtake – vieta-
 to sorpassare

do not pass – vietato
 sorpassare

doctor – il medico

dome – la cupola

door handle – la manig-
 lia della porta

door lock – la serratura
 della porta

downhill skiing – lo sci
 in discesa

dozen – la dozzina

drain – lo scarico

dress – il vestito

dried – essicato, secco

drill – il trapano

drinking water –
 l'acqua potabile

drive slowly – rallentare

driver's seat – il sedile
 del conducente

driving licence – la pa-
 tente

drops – le gocce

drugstore – la droghe-
 ria

dryer – l'essiccatrice

duck – l'anatra

(sand)dune – la duna

during the day – di gior-
 no/durante il giorno

during the evening – di
 sera

during the morning – di
 mattina

duty – la dogana

E

ear – l'orrechio

ear, nose and throat
 specialist – l'otorino-
 laringoiatra

Easter – Pasqua

egg(s) – l'uovo (sing.)
 le uova (plural)

eggplant – la melanza-
 na

elastic band – l'elastico

elastic lashing cord – il
 cavo flessibile

elbow – il gomito

electric drill – il trapano
 meccanico

electric shaver – il rasolo

electric tachometer – il
 contagiri elettrico

electrical goods shop –
 il negozio di articoli
 elettrici

elevator – l'ascensore

elm tree – l'olmo

emergency brake – il
 segnale d'allarme

engaged (telephone) –
 occupato

English garden – il gar-
 dino all'inglese

engraving – l'incisione
 su rame

escalator – le scale mo-
 bili

esophagus – l'esofago

estuary – la foce

evening – la sera

excavations – gli scavi

exclusion of liability – *l'esclusione di responsabilità*
exhaust pipe – *lo scappamento*
exhibition – *la mostra*
exit – *l'uscita*
express bus – *un autobus espresso*
express train – *il treno espresso*
express train – *il treno rapido*
eye – *l'occhio*
eye doctor – *l'oculista*
eyebrows – *le sopracciglie*
eyelid – *la palpebra*

F

fabric – *il tessuto, la stoffa*
face flannel – *lo strofinaccio per lavarsi*
facial – *la maschera*
factory – *la fabbrica*
falling rock – *caduta sassi*
fan – *la ventilazzione*
fast – *veloce*
February – *febbraio*
fees – *la tassa*
fender (car) – *il parafango*
fennel – *il finocchio*
fever – *la febbre*
figs – *i fichi*
finger(s) – *il dito (sing)/le dita (plu.)*
fingernail – *l'unghia*
first class – *la prima classe*
first name – *il prenome*

fish – *il pesce*
fish store – *la pescheria*
fishing – *pescare con l'amo*
fishing licence – *la licenza di pesca*
fishing line – *la lenza*
fishing permit – *la tessera di pesca*
fishing rod – *la canna da pesca*
flashlight – *la torcia*
flat tire – *il pneumatico sgonfio*
flight number – *il numero del volo*
flour – *la farina*
flu – *l'influenza*
fog lamps – *il fendinebbia*
food – *gli alimentari*
food allergy – *l'allergia da alimenti*
food poisoning – *l'intossicazione da alimenti*
foot – *il piede*
football (soccer) – *il calcio*
for – *per*
forest – *il bosco*
fork – *la forcella*
form – *il modulo*
fortress – *la fortezza*
four-lane – *a quattro corsie*
four-star petrol – *la (benzina) super*
four-wheel drive – *la trasmissione su tutte le ruote*
frame – *il telaio*
free, unoccupied – *libero*

fresh – *frescho*
fresh produce shop – *l'erbivendolo*
Friday – *venerdì*
fringe – *il pony*
frog – *la rana*
from – *di, da*
front wheel – *la ruota anteriore*
front-wheel drive – *la trazione anteriore*
fruit – *la frutta*
fruit stand – *il fruttivendolo*
fuel cap – *il tappo del serbatoio*
fuel filler neck – *il tappo della benzina*
fuel gauge – *l'indictatore del livello della benzina*
fuel pump – *la pompa, la colonna*
fuel tank ventilation – *l'aerazione del serbatoio*
full beard – *la barba piena*
fungal infection – *l'infezione micosa*
furniture – *i mobili*
furniture store – *il negozio di mobili*
fuse – *il fusibile (valvola)*

G

gallery – *il matroneo (theatre), la galeria (art)*
galoshes – *gli stivali di gomma*

game crossing – *selvaggina vagante*

garbage – *le immondizie*

garbage bag – *il sacchetto delle immondizie*

garbonzo beans – *i ceci*

garden – *il gardino*

gargoyle – *il doccione*

garlic – *l'aglio*

gas – *la benzina*

gas cartridge – *la bombola di gas*

gate – *il portone*

gate (airport) – *l'imbarco*

gear lever – *la leva del cambio*

gear shift – *il cambio di velocità*

German measles – *la rosolia*

given name – *il prenome*

(drinking) glass – *il bicchiere*

glass – *il vetro*

glasses – *gli occhiali*

gliding – *il volare a vela*

glove box – *il cassetto del cruscotto*

glove compartment – *il cassetto del cruscotto*

gloves – *i guanti*

glue – *la colla*

gnat – *la zanzara*

goat – *la capra*

golf club – *la mazza de golf*

golf course – *il golf*

Good Friday – *il venerdì santo*

goose – *l'oca*

Gothic – *il gotico*

gourmet food store – *il negozio di specialitá gastronomiche*

gramme – *il grammo*

grape – *il grappolo d'uva, l'uva*

grapefruit – *il pompelmo*

gravel – *la ghiaia*

Greeks – *i greci*

green – *verde*

green grocier – *l'erbivendolo*

green pepper – *il peperone*

grey – *grigio*

grilled – *alla griglia*

groceries – *gli alimentari*

grotto – *la grotta*

ground beef – *la carne macinata*

ground – *macinato*

gynecologist – *il ginecologo*

H

haemorrhoids – *le emorroidi*

hair – *i capelli*

hair curlers – *i bigodini*

hair dyeing – *colorare i capelli*

hair tinting – *tingere i capelli*

hair treatment – *il trattamento per i capelli*

hairbrush – *la spazzola per i capelli*

hairdresser – *il parruchiere*

hairdryer – *il casco asciugacapelli*

half-timber – *il traliccio*

hammer – *il martello*

hand(s) – *la mano (sing.)/le mani (pl.)*

hand brake – *il freno a mano*

handball – *la palla a mano*

handkerchief – *il fazzoletto*

handlebars – *il manubrio*

hang-gliding – *il deltaplano*

hard roll – *i panini*

hardware store – *il negozio di ferramenta*

hat – *il cappello*

hay fever – *la febbre da fieno*

hazard warning light – *la spia (luminosa)*

hazelnuts – *le nocciole*

head – *la testa*

head cushion – *il cuscino*

head lettuce – *la lattuga*

headache – *il mal di testa*

headlights – *la luce anteriore*

headrest – *il poggiatesta*

heart – *il cuore*

heater – *il riscaldamento*

heating – *il riscaldamento*

heatstroke – _il colpo di calore_
hectagramme – _l'etto_
helmet – _il casco_
help – _l'aiuto_
hematoma – _l'ematoma_
hemmoraging – _l'emorragia_
here you are – _prego_
herring – _l'aringa_
hexagonal socket head key – _la chiave esagonale_
highway – _l'autostrada_
high-beams – _la luce abbagliante_
hiking – _il camminare_
hill – _il colle_
holiday – _festivo_
hood (car) – _il cofano_
horse chestnut – _l'ippocastano_
horseback riding – _l'equitazione_
hose – _il tubo_
hospital – _l'ospedale_
hot peppers – _peproncini_
hotel – _l'albergo_
housewares – _gli articoli casalinghi_
how – _come_
however – _però_
hub – _il mozzo (della ruota)_
hunting – _la caccia_

I

ice – _ghiaccio_
ice skating – _il pattinaggio su ghiaccio_
if – _se_
ignition – _l'accensione_

ignition switch – _l'interruttore dell'accensione_
in front of – _davanti_
in the afternoon – _di pomeriggio_
in – _dentro, in_
information – _le informazioni_
insects – _gli insetti_
intestine – _l'intestino_
interference – _il guasto_
international health insurance form – _il modulo per una cura medica internazionale_
intersection – _l'incrocio, il quadrato_
intersection – _l'incrocio_
ironmonger – _il negozio di ferramenta_
ivory – _l'avorio_

J

(dress) jacket – _la giacca_
January – _gennaio_
jaundice – _l'itterizia_
jeans – _i jeans_
jellyfish – _la medusa_
jeweller – _la gioielleria_
juice – _il succo di frutta_
July – _luglio_
jumper – _il pullover, la maglia_
jumper cable – _il cavo di avviamento_
junction – _l'incrocio_
June – _guigno_

K

kerosin – _il petrolio_
key – _la chiave_

kidney – _il rene_
kilogramme – _il chilo_
kilometre – _il chilometro_
knee – _il ginocchio_
knife – _il coltello_

L

ladies' bicycle – _la bicicletta per donne_
ladies' suit – _il tailleur_
lagoon – _Il laguna_
lake – _il lago_
lamb – _l'agnello_
landscape – _il paesaggio_
laundrette – _la lavenderia_
laundromat – _la lavenderia_
laundry detergent – _il detersivo_
lava – _la lava_
lavatory – _la lavandino_
layered cut – _il taglio a gradini_
lead – _il piombo_
lead-free – _senza piombo_
leather – _la pelle_
leather goods – _la pelletteria_
leeks – _il porro_
lemon – _il limone_
lemonade – _la limonata_
lentils – _le lenticchie_
lettuce – _la lattuga_
level crossing – _passaggio a livello_
library – _la biblioteca_
lift – _l'ascensore_
light – _la luce_
light (colour) – _chiaro_
lightbulb – _la lampadina_
linens – _biancheria_

linens shop – *il nego-zoi di banchieria*

lingerie – *la biancheria intima*

lining – *la fodera*

litre – *il litro*

lizard – *la lucertola*

local train – *il treno locale*

loose chippings – *pietrisco*

loose gravel – *pietrisco*

lorry – *autocarro*

low-beams – *la luce schermata*

luggage – *i bagagli*

luggage counter – *lo sportello accettazio-ne bagagli*

luggage locker – *il de-posito bagagli a cas-sette*

luggage rack – *la rete portabagagli*

lumbago – *la lombaggi-ne*

lunch – *il pranzo*

lung – *il polmone*

▓ M ▓

magazine – *la rivista,il periodico*

maiden name – *il nome da nubile*

(first/second) main course – *il primo/ se-condo platto*

main wash cycle – *il la-vaggio*

maize – *il mais*

make-up – *truccare*

malaria – *la malaria*

manicure – *il manicure*

manorhouse – *la villa (signorile)*

maple – *l'acero*

marble – *il marmo*

March – *marzo*

marjoram – *la mag-giorana*

market – *il mercato*

massage – *il massag-gio*

matches – *i fiammiferi*

material – *il tessuto, la stoffa*

May – *maggio*

mayonnaise – *la maio-nese*

meadow – *il prato*

measles – *il morbillo*

meat – *la carne*

Mediterranean – *il Me-diterraneo*

(honeydew) melon – *il melone*

menstrual pain – *i dolo-ri degli organi genita-li femminili*

menstruation – *le mestruazioni*

menu – *la lista*

men's bicycle – *la bicicletta per uomini*

men's clothing – *l'ab-bigliamento per uomi-ni*

metre – *il metro*

metre stick – *il metro*

(during) midday, noon – *(a)/il mezzogiorno*

middle, centre – *il centro*

Middle Ages – *il me-dioevo*

middle ear infection – *l'otite media*

migraine – *l'emicrania*

milk – *il latte*

minced meat – *la car-ne macinata*

miniature golf – *il mini-golf*

mint – *la menta*

mirror – *lo specchio*

modern times – *l'età moderna*

Monday – *il lunedì*

moped – *il ciclomotore*

morning – *la mattina*

mosaic – *il mosaico*

mosque – *la moschea*

mosquito – *la zanzara*

motor scooter – *il moto-rino*

motor sport – *il motoris-mo*

motorcycle – *la mo-tocicletta*

motorway – *l'autostra-da*

mouldy – *ammuffito*

mountain – *il monte*

mountain bike – *la mo-untainbike*

mountain climbing – *l'alpinismo*

mountain range (mas-sif) – *il massiccio*

mountain range – *le montagne*

moustache – *i baffi*

mudflats – *il bassofon-do*

mudguard (bicycle) – *il parafango*

mug – *la coppa*

mumps – *la parotite*

municipal bus – *l'auto-
bus urbano*
museum – *il museo*
mussels – *le cozze*
mustard – *il senape*

N

nail – *il chiodo*
nail file – *la limetta da
unghie*
name – *il nome*
nappies – *i pannolini*
national holiday – *festa
nazionale*
national park – *il parco
nazionale*
nationality – *la nazionalitá*
nausea – *il giramento i
stomaco*
nave – *la navata*
near – *vicino*
neck – *il collo*
neck scarf – *la sciarpa
da collo*
nerves – *i nervi*
New Year – *capodanno*
news agent – *il gior-
nalaio*
newspaper – *il giornale*
newsstand – *il gior-
nalaio*
next – *prossimo(a)*
night – *la notte*
nightshirt – *la camicia
de notte*
nine-pin bowling – *il
gioco de birilli*
no parking – *divieto di
parcheggio*
no stopping – *divieto di
sosta*
no – *no*

non-smoking – *vietato
fumare*
noodles – *le paste*
nose – *il naso*
nosebleed – *l'emorra-
gia nasale*
November – *novembre*
nutmeg – *la noce mo-
scata*
nuts – *le noci*
nylons – *le calze di ny-
lon*

O

oak – *la querica*
observatory – *l'osser-
vatorio*
occupation – *la profes-
sione*
occupied – *occupato*
ocean – *il mare*
October – *ottobre*
off-road vehicle – *il veicolo per marcia fuori
strada*
oil – *l'olio*
oil pan – *la coppa
dell'olio*
oil pump – *la pompa
dell'olio*
ointment – *la pomata*
olives – *le olive*
on – *su*
oncoming traffic – *il
traffico in senso
contrario*
one-lane – *a una corsia*
one-way flight – *il volo
di andata*
one-way street – *sen-
so unico*
onions – *le cipolle*
open carriage – *il gran-
de vagone*

optician – *l'ottico*
or – *o*
orange (colour) – *aran-
cione*
orange (fruit) – *l'arancia*
oregano – *l'origano*
othopaedic surgeon –
l'ortopedico
outside mirror – *lo
specchietto esterno*

P

package – *il pacco/*
packet — *il pacchetto*
packing cord – *le cing-
hie*
paediatrician – *il pediatra*
pain reliever – *il cal-
mante*
painting – *il quadro, il
dipito*
Palm Sunday – *la do-
menica delle palme*
pannier bag – *il tasca-
pane per bicicletta*
panorama – *il panora-
ma*
panty hose – *il collant*
parachuting – *il paraca-
dutismo*
paraffin – *il petrolio*
paragliding – *parapen-
dio*
pardon? – *come?*
parking disc – *disco or-
ario*
parking lights – *la luce
di posizione*
parking meter – *parchi-
metro*
parsley – *il prezzemolo*
passenger car – *auto-
vettura*

passenger seat – *il sedile a fianco del conduttore*
pasta – *le paste*
pastries – *i biscotti*
pastry shop – *la pasticceria*
peach – *la pesca*
peanuts – *le noccioline americane*
pear – *la pera*
peas – *i piselli*
pedal – *il pedale*
pedal brake – *il freno a contrepedale*
pedestal – *il piedistallo*
pedicure – *il pedicure*
Pentecost – *Pentecoste*
pepper – *il pepe*
perm(anent) – *la permanente*
petrol – *la benzina*
pharmacy – *la farmacia*
phillip's head screwdriver – *il cacciavite a croce*
physician – *il medico*
pickles – *i certicoli sott'aceto*
picture – *il dipito*
pig – *il maiale*
pigeon – *il piggione*
pike – *il luccio*
pillar – *il pilastro*
pillow – *il cuscino*
pine – *il pino*
pineapple – *l'ananas*
ping-pong – *il tennis da tavolo*
pink – *rosa*
pipe wrench – *le pinze per tubi*
pistachios – *i pistacchi*

place – *il luogo*
place of birth – *il luogo di nascita*
place of issue (passport) – *il luogo di emissione*
place of residence – *il luogo di residenza*
place setting – *il coperto*
plane tree – *il platano*
plaster (adhesive strip) – *il cerotto*
plastercast – *l'ingessatura*
plate – *il piatto*
plaza – *la piazza*
please – *per favore*
pliers – *le tenaglie*
plum – *la prugna*
pocket lamp – *la torcia*
pond – *lo stagno*
poplar – *il pioppo*
porcelain – *la porcellana*
pork – *il maiale*
portal – *il portale*
potatoes – *le patate*
potholes – *buche*
pound (metric), 500 g – *il mezzo chilo*
powder – *la cipria*
premium gas – *la (benzina) super*
prescription – *la prescrizione*
pre-wash cycle – *il prelavaggio*
price – *il prezzo*
print – *la stampa*
programme – *il programma*
prohibited – *vietato*

promontory – *lo spuntone*
pulled tendon – *lo stiramento del tendine*
pullover – *la maglia, il pullover*
pump – *la pompa*
puncture repair kit – *il corredo per riprazione di forature*
purple – *lilla*
purse – *la borsa*
pyjama – *il pigiama*

Q

quail – *la quaglia*
quicksand – *la sabbia mobile*
quince – *la cotogna*

R

rabbit – *il coniglio*
radar check – *il controllo radar*
radiator – *il radiatore*
radio – *la radio*
radish – *il rafano*
radish (small) – *il ravanello*
rain cape, rain jacket, raincoat – *l'impermeabile*
raisin – *l'uva secca*
rapids – *la cateratta*
rash – *l'eruzione cutanea*
raspberries – *i lamponi*
ravine – *il precipizio*
raw – *crudo*
razor blades – *le lame*
rear fog lamps – *il faro posteriore fendinebbia*

rear-view mirror – *il retrovisore*

rear wheel – *la ruota posteriore*

rear-wheel drive – *la trazione posteriore*

receipt – *la ricevuta*

reception – *la recezione*

red – *rosso*

red beets – *la barbabietola rossa*

reeds – *le canne*

refill the coolant – *rimettere l'acqua nel radiatore*

reflector – *il rifletorre*

Renaissance – *il rinascimento*

rental period – *la durata del noleggio*

reservation – *la prenotazione*

reservoir – *il lago artificiale*

restaurant car – *il vagone-ristorante*

return flight – *il volo di ritorno*

reversed charges – *la telefonata R*

rib – *la costola*

rice – *il riso*

ricotta cheese – *la ricotta*

river – *il fiume*

rivet – *il rivetto*

road – *la strada, la via*

road narrows – *strettoia*

rock – *la roccia*

rolled oats – *fiocchi d'avena*

(hard) rolls – *i panini*

Romanesque – *il romanico*

Romans – *i romani*

Romantic (period) – *il romanticismo*

roof – *il tetto*

rosemary – *il rosmarino*

rotten – *guasto*

rough stone – *un frammento di pietra*

roundabout – *la rotonda*

row – *la fila*

rowboat – *la barca a remi*

rubber – *la gomma*

rubbing alcohol – *lo spirito*

rubbish – *le immondizie*

rubbish bag – *il sacchetto delle immondizie*

rubella – *la rosolia*

ruin(s) – *la rovina*

runner beans – *il fagiolo*

rye – *la segala*

S

safety pin – *la spilla di sicurezza*

saffron – *lo zafferano*

sage – *la salvia*

sailing – *navigare a vela*

salmonella poisoning – *l'avvelenamento di salmonelle*

salt – *il sale*

sand – *la sabbia*

sand bank – *il banco di sabbia*

sandals – *i sandali*

sandpaper – *la carta abrasiva*

sanitary napkins – *gli assorbenti*

sarcophagus – *il sarcofago*

Saturday – *sabato*

sauna – *la sauna*

sausage – *la salsiccia*

sausages – *le salsiccette*

saw – *la sega*

scarf (neck) – *il fazzoletto*

scarf (winter) – *il foulard*

scenic overlook – *il belvedere*

schedule – *l'orario*

school – *la scuola*

sciatica – *l'ischialgia*

scissors – *le forbici*

scorpion – *lo scorpione*

Scotch pine – *il pino silvestre*

scouring powder – *l'abrasivo*

screw – *la vite*

screwdriver – *il cacciavite*

scuba diving – *l'immersione*

sculpture – *la scultura*

sculptures – *le sculture*

sea urchin – *il riccio di mare*

sea – *il mare*

seafood – *i frutti di mare*

seagull – *il gabbiano*

seam – *l'orlo*

seat – *il posto, la sella*

seatback – *la spalliera*

second class – *la seconda classe*

second-hand book store – *la libreria antiquaria*

second-hand shop – *il rigattiere*

self-service – *self-service*

September – *settembre*

service – *il servizio*

sewing machine oil – *l'olio per le macchine per cucire*

sewing needle – *l'ago (per cucire)*

shampoo – *la shampoo*

shaving brush – *il pennello da barba*

shaving soap – *il sapone de barba*

shell – *la conchiglia*

shin – *lo stinco*

shirt – *la camicia*

shivering fit – *i brividi di febbre*

shock absorber – *l'ammortizzatore*

shoe shop – *il negozio di calzature*

shoelace – *il laccio per scarpe*

shoes – *le scarpe*

shopping bag – *la borsa, il sacchetto, la tascha*

shorts – *i pantaloncini corti, gli shorts*

shower – *la doccia*

shrubs – *la boscaglia*

sick-fund – *la cassa mutua*

side aisles – *la navata laterale*

sideburns (long) – *i basettoni*

sideburns – *le basette*

signature – *la firma*

sill – *la cornice*

silverware – *le posate*

sink – *il lavello*

ski binding – *gli attacchi*

ski instructor – *il maestro/la maestra di sci*

ski lift – *lo ski-lift*

ski suit – *la tenuta da sci*

ski wax – *la sciolina*

skiing – *lo sciare*

skiing lessons – *il corso di sci*

skin – *la pelle*

skirt – *la gonna*

skis – *gli sci*

skittles – *il gioco de birilli*

slacks – *i pantaloni*

slate – *l'ardesia*

sledding – *la slitta*

sleeper car – *il vagone letto*

sleeping pills – *il sonnifero*

sleeve – *la manica*

sleveless sweater – *il pullover senza maniche*

slice (of salami) – *la fetta (di salame)*

sliced – *tagliato a fette*

slipover – *il pullover senza maniche*

slippery road – *strada sdrucciolevole*

slow – *lento*

smoking – *fumatori*

snack – *la qualcosa*

snail, escargo – *la lumacha*

snake – *il serpente*

snorkel – *il tubo di respirazione*

soaking solution (contact lenses) – *la soluzione per la conservazione*

soap – *il sapone*

soccer – *il calcio*

social medical fund – *la casa mutua*

socks – *i calzini*

soft drink – *la limonata*

solarium – *il banco abbronzante*

sore throat – *il mal di gola*

sound (geol.) – *il sund*

soup – *la zuppa*

sour cream – *la panna da cucina*

sour – *acido*

spanner – *la chiave (per dadi)*

spare wheel – *la ruota di scorta*

sparking plug – *la candale d'ascensione*

sparkplug – *la candale d'ascensione*

spectacles – *gli occhiali*

speed limit – *limitazione della velocità*

speedometer – *il tachimetro*

spinach – *lo spinacio*

spirits – *lo spirito*

spoiled – *guasto*

spokes – *i raggi*

sporting goods – *gli articoli sportivi*

sprain – *la slogatura*

spring (season) – *la primavera*

spring (water) – *la sorgente*

spruce – *l'abete rosso*

square – *la piazza*

squash – *la zucca*

stain – *la macchia*

stairs – *le scale*

stalls (theatre) – *le prime file della platea*

starter – *il dispositivo d'avviamento*

starter/appetizer – *l'antipasto*

station restaurant – *il ristorante della stazione*

stationery shop – *la cartoleria*

stationery – *la carta da lettere*

statue – *la statua*

steamed – *stufato*

steering wheel – *il volante*

steering wheel lock – *il bloccasterzo*

stickshift – *la leva del cambio*

stockings – *le calze*

stomach – *lo stomaco*

stomach ache – *il mal di ventre*

stone – *la pietra*

stop – *alt*

straight on, ahead – *sempre diritto*

strait – *lo stretto*

strawberries – *le fragole*

stream – *il ruscello*

street – *la strada, la via*

string beans – *il fagiolo*

striped – *a strisce*

stripping knife – *la spatola*

sugar – *lo zucchero*

summer – *l'estate*

sunburn – *la scottatura solare*

Sunday – *la domenica*

sunglasses – *gli occhiali ba sole*

sunhat – *il cappello da sole*

sunstroke – *l'insolazione*

suntan oil – *l'olio solare*

supper – *la cena*

surfing – *praticare il surfing*

surgeon – *il chirugo*

sweater – *la maglia, il pullover*

sweating – *la traspirazione*

sweet chestnut – *il castagno*

sweet pepper – *il peperone*

sweet – *dolce*

sweets – *i dolci*

swimsuit – *il costume de bagno*

swimming – *il nuoto*

swimming trunks – *i calzoncini de bagno*

synagogue – *la sinagoga*

T

table – *il tavolo*

table tennis – *il tennis da tavolo*

tablespoon – *il cucchiaio*

tablets – *le compresse*

tail lights – *la luce posteriore*

tailor – *la sartoria*

tampon – *il tampone*

tank – *il serbatoio*

tarragon – *l'estragone*

tea – *il té*

teaspoon – *il cucchiaino*

telephone – *il telefono*

telephone book – *l'elenco telefonico*

telephone box/booth – *la cabina telefonica*

telephone fee unit – *lo scatto*

telephone number – *il numero dell'abbonato*

telephone service department – *l'ufficio guasti*

television – *il televisore*

temple – *il tempio*

tennis – *il tennis*

tennis court – *il campo de tennis*

tennis racket – *la racchetta (da tennis)*

tent – *la tenda*

tent peg – *il picchetto*

tent pole – *il palo da tenda*

ten-speed bicycle – *la bicicletta a dieci velocità*

tetanus – *il tetano*

thank you – *grazie*

theatre – *il teatro*

thermometer – *il termometro*

this evening – *stasera*

this morning – *stamattina*

thread – *il filo per cucire*

three-speed bicycle – *la bicicletta a tre velocità*

throat – *la gola*

through – *attraverso*

thumb – *il pollice*

Thursday – *giovedì*

thyme – *il timo*

ticket – *il biglietto*

ticket check – *il controllo biglietti*

ticket checker – *il controllore/la controllatrice*

tie – *la cravatta*

timetable – *l'orario*

tin – *la lattina*

tincture – *la tintura*

tire – *il pneumatico, la gomma*

tire pressure – *la pressione delle gomme*

to (a place) – *fino a*

to check the oil level – *controliare il livello dell'olio*

to clean – *pulire a secco*

to dance – *ballare*

to iron – *stirare*

to the back – *dietro*

to the left – *a sinistra*

to the right – *a destra*

to wash – *lavare*

toad – *il rospo*

tobacco – *il tabacco*

tobacconist – *la tabaccheria*

today – *oggi*

toe – *il dito del piede*

toilet, WC – *il gabinetto*

toilet paper – *la carta igienica*

toll (motorway/highway) – *pedaggio (autostradale)*

tomatoes – *i pomodori*

tomorrow – *domani*

tomorrow evening – *domani sera*

tongue – *la lingua*

tonsilitis – *la tonsillite*

too – *anche*

tool box – *la cassetta portautensil*

tooth – *il dente*

toothache – *il mal di denti*

toothbrush – *lo spazzolino da denti*

toothpaste – *il dentifricio*

torn ligament – *lo strappo*

torn muscle – *lo strappo muscolare*

tortoiseshell – *il corno*

toupet – *il toupet*

towel – *l'asciugamano*

tower – *il torre*

towing cable – *il cavo da rimorchio*

toy store – *il negozio di gioccattoli*

track (train)– *il binario*

traffic circle – *la circolazione rotatario*

traffic circle – *la rotonda*

traffic light – *il semaforo*

trail – *la pista*

trailer – *rimorchio*

train platform – *il marciapiede*

train station – *la stazione*

train wagon, carriage – *la carrozza*

transepts – *l'edificio traversale*

transmission – *il cambio*

treatment room – *lo studio medico*

tree – *l'albero*

trousers – *i pantaloni*

trout – *la trota*

truck – *autocarro*

trunk (car) – *il portabagagli*

trunk code – *il prefisso telefonico*

tube – *il tubo*

Tuesday – *martedì*

turkey – *la tacchina*

turn signal – *le freccie*

turn signal switch – *il lampeggiatore*

two-lane – *a due corsie*

T-shirt – *il T-shirt*

U

umbrella – *l'ombrello*

under – *sotto*

underpants – *le mutande*

undershirt – *la maglietta*

underwear – *la biancheria intima*

unleaded – *senza piombo*

unlimited mileage – *il forfait chilometrico*
until – *finchè*
usher/usherette – *la maschera*

V

vacation – *le vacanzae*
vaccination – *la vaccinazione*
vaccination certification – *il certificato di vaccinazione*
valley – *la valle*
valve – *la valvola*
veal – *il vitello*
vegetables – *le verdure*
vessel – *il recipiente*
vest – *il panciotto, il gil*
viewpoint – *il belvedere*
vinegar – *l'aceto*
vineyards – *i vigneti*
viper – *la vipera*
volcano – *il vulcano*
volleyball – *la pallavolo*
vomiting – *il vomito*

W

wagon number (train) – *il numero della carrozza*
waiter – *il cameriere*
waiting hall – *la sala d'attesa*
waiting room – *l'anticamera*
waitress – *la cameriera*
wall – *il muro*
walnut – *la noce*
warning light – *la lampada di controllo*
washcloth – *lo strofinaccio per lavarsi*

washer – *la rosetta*
washing machine – *la lavatrice*
washing powder – *il detersivo*
washroom – *la lavandino*
watch – *l'orologio*
watchmaker – *l'orologiaio*
water – *l'acqua*
water canister – *il bidone dell'acqua*
water skiing – *lo sci acquatico*
waterfall – *la cascata*
watermelon – *il coccomero*
Wednesday – *mercoledì*
week – *la settimana*
weeping willow – *il salice piangente*
wellingtons – *gli stivali di gomma*
wet – *umido*
what? – *che cosa?*
wheat – *il grano*
wheel rim – *il cerchione*
wheel – *la ruota*
when? – *quando?*
whipping cream – *la panne dolce*
white – *bianco*
who – *chi*
wig – *la parrucca*
wild boar – *il cinghiale*
willow – *il salice*
window – *la finestra*
window seat – *un posto accanto al finestrino*

windscreen, windshield – *il parabrezza*
windscreen wipers – *il tergicristallo*
windshield wipers – *il tergicristallo*
wine – *il vino*
wine shop – *il negozio di vini*
wing (car) – *il parafango*
winter – *l'inverno*
winter scarf – *il foulard*
wire – *il filo*
with – *con*
without – *senza*
women's clothing – *l'abbigliamento per donne*
wood – *il legno*
wool – *la lana*
wound – *la ferita*
wrench – *la chiave (per dadi)*
writing paper – *la carta da lettere*

Y

year – *l'anno*
yellow pages – *l'elenco telefonico per categorie, le pagine gialle*
yellow – *giallo*
yes – *si*
yesterday – *ieri*
yogurt – *il iogurt*

Z

zip(per) – *la chiusura lampo*
zoo – *lo zoo*
zucchini – *le zucchine*

Glossary

Italian — English

A

l'abazia – *abbey*

l'abbigliamento per bambini – *children's clothing*

l'abbigliamento per donne – *women's clothing*

l'abbigliamento per uomini – *men's clothing*

l'abete rosso – *spruce*

l'abrasivo – *scouring powder, clenser*

l'accappatoio – *bathrobe*

l'accendino – *cigarette lighter*

l'accensione – *ignition*

le acciuge – *anchovies*

l'acero – *maple*

l'aceto – *vinegar*

acido – *sour*

l'acqua – *water*

l'acqua potabile – *drinking water*

l'acquaedotto – *water line/aqueduct*

l'acquario – *aquarium*

gli adulti – *adults*

l'aerazione del serbatoio – *fuel tank ventilation*

l'aeroporto – *airport*

l'agenzia di noleggio di automobili – *car rental agency*

l'aglio – *garlic*

l'agnello – *lamb*

l'ago (per cucire) – *sewing needle*

agosto – *August*

l'aiuto – *help*

l'albero – *tree*

l'albero a camme – *camshaft*

l'albero a gomiti – *crankshaft*

l'albergo – *hotel*

le albicocche – *apricots*

gli alimentari – *food, groceries*

l'alimentazione infantile – *baby food*

alla griglia – *grilled*

l'allergia da alimenti – *food allergy*

l'alpinismo – *mountain climbing*

alt – *stop*

l'altare – *altar*

l'ambra – *amber*

l'ammortizzatore – *shock absorber*

ammuffito – *mouldy*

l'ananas – *pineapple*

l'anatra – *duck*

anche – *also, too*

l'aneto – *dill*

l'anice – *anis*

gli animali – *animals*

l'anno – *year*

l'anticamera – *waiting room*

l'antichità – *antiquity*

le antichità – *antiques*

l'antipasto – *starter/appetizer*

l'appartamento – *apartment*

l'appendice – *appendix*

l'apribottiglie – *bottle opener*

aprile – *April*

l'apriscatole – *can opener*

l'arancia – *orange (fruit)*

arancione – *orange (colour)*

l'arbusto – *bush, shrub*

l'ardesia – *slate*

l'argilla – *clay*

l'aria condzionata – *air conditioning*

l'aringa – *herring*

l'arrivo – *arrival*

gli articoli casalinghi – *housewares*

gli articoli sportivi – *sporting goods*

l'ascensore – *lift, elevator*

l'asciugamano – *towel*

asciugare con l'asiugacapelli – *blow drying*

l'asparago – *asparagus*

l'asse – *axle*

l'asse di supporto – *axle bearing*

l'assicurazione con copertura totale – *comprehensive insurance*

gli assorbenti – *sanitary napkins*

gli attacchi – *ski binding*

attenzione – *attention, caution*

attenzione al treno – *caution train*

attraverso – *through*

un autobus espresso – *express bus*

l'autobus interurbano – *cross-country bus*
l'autobus urbano – *municipal bus*
l'autocaravan – *caravan, camping vehicle, RV*
autocarro – *lorry, truck*
l'auotradio – *car radio*
l'autostrada – *motorway, highway*
autovettura – *passenger car*
l'autunno – *autumn, fall*
l'avorio – *ivory*
l'avvelenamento di salmonelle – *salmonella poisoning*
azzurro – *blue*

B

i baffi – *moustache*
i bagagli – *luggage, bags*
il bagno – *bathroom*
la baia – *bay*
il balcone – *balcony*
ballare – *to dance, dancing*
i bambini – *children*
la banana – *banana*
il banco – *bank*
il banco abbronzante – *solarium*
il banco di sabbia – *sand bank*
la barba – *beard*
la barba piena – *full beard*
la barbabietola rossa – *red beets*
il barbiere – *barber*
la barca a remi – *rowboat*

il barocco – *baroque*
le basette – *sideburns*
i basettoni – *long sideburns*
la basilica – *basilica*
il basilico – *basil*
il bassofondo – *mudflats*
la batteria (automotive) – *battery*
beige – *beige*
il belvedere – *scenic overlook, viewpoint*
la benda – *bandage*
la benzina – *petrol, gas*
la (benzina) super – *four-star petrol, premium gas*
il berretto – *cap*
la betulla – *birch*
la bevande – *beverages*
biancheria – *linens*
la biancheria intima – *lingerie, underwear*
bianco – *white*
la biblioteca – *library*
il bicchiere – *(drinking) glass*
la bicicletta a dieci velocità – *ten-speed bicycle*
la bicicletta a tre velocità – *three-speed bicycle*
la bicicletta per donne – *ladies' bicycle*
la bicicletta per uomini – *men's bicycle*
il bidone dell'acqua – *water canister*
il biglietto – *ticket*
i bigodini – *hair curlers*

il binario – *train track*
la birra – *beer*
i biscotti – *pastries, biscuits, cookies*
il blazer – *blazer*
il bloccasterzo – *steering wheel lock*
blu – *blue*
la blusa – *blouse*
la bolla – *blister*
bollito – *boiled*
la bombola di gas – *gas cartridage*
la borsa – *shopping bag, purse*
la boscaglia – *shrubs*
il bosco – *forest*
il bottone – *button*
il braccio (sing.) le braccia (pl.) – *arm*
i brividi di febbre – *shivering fit*
broccoli – *broccoli*
i bronchi – *bronchial tubes*
la bronchite – *bronchitis*
il bronzo – *bronze*
buche – *potholes*
il burro – *butter*
la busta/il sacchetto – *bag*

C

la cabina telefonica – *telephone box, booth*
la caccia – *hunting*
il cacciavite – *screwdriver*
il cacciavite a croce – *cross-point screwdriver, phillip's head screwdriver*
caduta sassi – *falling rock*

il caffé – *coffee*

il calcio – *football, soccer*

il callo – *corn (on foot)*

il calmante – *pain reliever*

le calze – *stockings*

i calzini – *socks*

i calzoncini de bagno – *swimming trunks*

il cambio – *transmission*

il cambio di velocità – *gear shift*

la cameriera – *waitress, chambermaid*

il cameriere – *waiter*

la camicetta – *blouse*

la camicia – *shirt*

la camicia de notte – *nightshirt*

il camminare – *hiking*

il campanello – *bell*

il campanile – *church tower*

il camping/il campeggio – *camping area*

il campo de tennis – *tennis court*

il canale – *canal*

la candale d'ascensione – *sparking plug, sparkplug*

la canna da pesca – *fishing rod*

la canna palustre/le canne – *reeds, cane*

la canoa – *canoeing*

cantiere – *construction zone*

la capella – *chapel*

i capelli – *hair*

il capitello – *capital (of column)*

capodanno – *New Year*

il cappello – *hat*

il cappello da sole – *sunhat*

i capperi – *capers*

il cappotto – *coat*

la capra – *goat*

la capsula – *capsule*

il carbine de grill – *charcoal*

il carburatore – *carburettor*

il carciofo – *artichoke*

la carne – *meat*

la carne macinata – *minced meat, ground beef*

il carnevale – *Carneval*

le carote – *carrots*

la carpa – *carp*

il carrello – *chasis*

la carrozza – *train car, carriage*

la carrozza con cuccete – *couchette car*

la carrozzeria – *body (of car)*

la carta abrasiva – *sandpaper*

la carta da lettere – *writing paper, stationery*

la carta igienica – *toilet paper*

la cartoleria – *stationery shop*

la cascata – *waterfall*

il casco – *helmet*

il casco asciugacapelli – *hairdryer*

la cassa mutua – *social medical fund, sick-fund*

la cassetta portautensil – *tool box*

il cassetto del cruscotto – *glove box, glove compartment*

le castagne – *chestnuts*

il castagno – *sweet chestnut*

il castello – *castle*

la cantena – *chain*

la cateratta – *rapids*

la cauzione – *caution*

il cavatappi – *corkscrew*

la caverna – *cave, cavern*

il cavo – *cable*

il cavo da rimorchio – *towing cable*

il cavo di avviamento – *jumper cable*

il cavo flessibile – *elastic lashing cord*

il cavolfiore – *cauliflower*

i cavolini di Bruxelles – *Brussels sprouts*

il cavolo – *cabbage*

i ceci – *chickpeas, garbonzo beans*

la cena – *supper*

il centimetro – *centimetre*

la centrale telefonica – *central telephone switchboard*

il centro – *middle, centre*

la ceramica – *ceramics*

il cerchione – *wheel rim*

il cerfoglio – *chervil*

il cerotto – *plaster, band-aid*

il certificato di vaccinazione – *vaccination certification*

cervi – *deer*

il cespuglio – *bush*

il cestino della bicicletta – *bicycle basket*

i certicoli sott'aceto – *pickles*

il cetriolo – *cucumber*

che – *what, that*

chi – *who*

chiaro – *light (colour)*

la chiave – *key*

la chiave (per dadi) – *spanner, wrench*

la chiave esagonale – *hexagonal socket head key*

la chiesa – *church*

il chilo – *kilogramme*

il chilometro – *kilometre*

il chiodo – *nail*

il chiostro – *cloister*

il chirugo – *surgeon*

la chiusura lampo – *zip(per)*

il ciclismo – *cycling*

il ciclista – *cyclist*

il ciclomotore – *moped*

la cicoria di Bruxelles – *chickory*

le cigliege – *cherries*

il cimitero – *cemetery*

le cinghie – *packing cord*

il cinghiale – *wild boar*

la cioccolata – *chocolate*

le cipolle – *onions*

il cipresso – *cypress*

la cipria – *powder*

la circolazione rotatorio – *traffic circle*

la cistite – *bladder infection*

la città – *city*

il classicismo – *classicism*

il clima – *climate*

il coccio – *brick*

il coccomero – *watermelon*

il cofano – *bonnet, hood (of car)*

la colla – *glue*

il collant – *stockings, nylons*

il colle – *hill*

il colletto – *collar*

la colonna – *fuel pump*

le colonne – *columns*

colorare i capelli – *hair dyeing*

colorato – *colourful*

a colori – *coloured*

il colpo di calore – *heatstroke*

il coltello – *knife*

come? – *pardon?*

come – *how*

la commozione cerebrale – *concussion*

il commutatore delle luci – *dimmer switch*

la compressa – *compress*

le compresse – *tablets*

con – *with*

la conchiglia – *shell*

il conduttore dell'acqua del radiatore – *coolant hose*

il coniglio – *rabbit*

il contagiri elettrico – *electric tachometer*

il conto – *bill*

il contrafforte – *beams (structural)*

contro – *against*

controliare il livelio dell'olio – *to check the oil level*

il controllo biglietti – *ticket check*

il controllo radar – *radar check*

il controllore/la controllatrice – *ticket checker*

la contusione – *contusion, bruise*

il coperchio del portabagagli – *boot/trunk lid*

la coperta – *blanket*

il coperto – *place setting*

la coppa – *mug*

la coppa dell'olio – *oil pan*

la cornice – *sill*

il corno – *tortoiseshell*

il coro – *choir*

Corpus Domini – *Corpus Christi*

il corredo per riprazione di forature – *puncture repair kit*

il corridoio – *corridor*

a una corsia – *one-lane*

a due corsie – *two-lane*

a quattro corsie – *four-lane*

il corso di sci – *skiing lessons*

la costipazione – *constipation*
la costola – *rib*
il costume di bagno – *swimsuit*
il costume di bagno a due pezzi (bikini) – *two-piece bathing suit, bikini*
la cotogna – *quince*
il cotone – *cotton*
le cozze – *mussels*
il crampo – *cramp*
la cravatta – *tie*
la cripta – *crypt*
la croce – *cross*
crudo – *raw*
il cucchiaino – *teaspoon*
il cucchiaio – *tablespoon*
la cuffia de bagno – *bathing cap*
il cuore – *heart*
la cupola – *dome*
la curva – *curve*
il cuscinetto a sfere – *ball bearing*
il cuscino – *head cushion, pillow*

D

da – *from*
il danno – *damage*
la data – *date*
la data di emissione – *date of issue*
la data di entrata/di uscita – *date of entry/departure*
la data di nascita – *date of birth*
i datteri – *dates*
davanti – *in front of*

il deltaplano – *hang-gliding*
il dente – *tooth*
il dentifricio – *toothpaste*
il dentista – *dentist*
dentro – *in*
il deodorante – *deoderant*
il deposito bagagli a cassette – *luggage locker*
il dermatologo – *dermatologist*
il deserto – *desert*
il dessert – *dessert*
a destra – *to the right*
il detersivo – *washing powder, laundry detergent*
il detersivo per le stoviglie – *dish washing liquid*
deviazione – *deversion, detour*
di giorno/durante il giorno – *during the day*
la diarrea – *diarrhoea*
dicembre – *December*
dietro – *to the back, behind*
difficoltà di respiro – *breathing difficulties*
il dipito – *painting, picture*
disco orario – *parking disc*
il dispositivo d'avviamento – *starter*
il dito (sing)/le dita (plu.) – *finger(s)*
il dito del piede – *toes*
divieto di parcheggio – *no parking*

divieto di sosta – *no stopping*
la doccia – *shower*
il doccione – *gargoyle*
la dogana – *duty, customs*
dolce – *sweet*
il dolce – *sweet, dessert*
i dolci – *sweets, candy*
i dolori alla schiena – *backache*
i dolori articolari – *aching joints*
i dolori degli organi genitali femminili – *menstrual pain*
domani – *tomorrow*
domani sera – *tomorrow evening*
la domenica – *Sunday*
la domenica delle palme – *Palm Sunday*
dopo – *after*
dopo domani – *day after tomorrow*
la dozzina – *dozen*
la drogheria – *drugstore*
la duna – *(sand)dune*
la durata del noleggio – *rental period*

E

e – *and*
l'edificio – *building*
l'edificio annesso – *annex (of a building)*
l'edificio traversale – *transepts*
l'elastico – *elastic band*
l'elenco telefonico – *telephone book*

l'elenco telefonico per categorie – *yellow pages*

l'ematoma – *hematoma*

l'emicrania – *migraine*

l'emorragia – *hemmoraging*

l'emorragia nasale – *nosebleed*

le emorroidi – *haemorrhoids*

l'equitazione – *horseback riding*

l'erba cipolina – *chives*

l'erbivendolo – *green grocier, fresh produce shop*

l'eruzione cutanea – *rash*

l'esclusione di responsabilità – *exclusion of liability*

l'esofago – *esophagus*

essicato – *dried*

l'essiccatrice – *dryer*

l'estate – *summer*

l'estragone – *tarragon*

l'etto – *hectagramme*

l'età – *age*

l'età moderna – *modern times*

F

la fabbrica – *factory*

il faggio – *beech tree*

i fagioli – *beans*

il fagiolo – *string beans*

la farina – *flour*

la farmacia – *pharmacy*

il faro posteriore fendinebbia – *rear fog lamps*

la fascia – *bandage*

la fasciatura – *bandage*

la fava – *beans*

il fazzoletto – *handkerchief, scarf*

febbraio – *February*

la febbre – *fever*

la febbre da fieno – *hay fever*

il fendinebbia – *fog lamps*

la ferita – *wound*

la fermata – *bus stop*

festa nazionale – *national holiday*

festivo – *holiday*

la fetta (di salame) – *slice (of salami)*

i fiammiferi – *matches*

i fichi – *figs*

la fila – *row*

il filo – *wire*

il filo per cucire – *thread*

finchè – *until*

la finestra – *window*

fino a – *to (a place)*

il finocchio – *fennel*

fiocchi d'avena – *rolled oats*

la firma – *signature*

il fiume – *river*

la foce – *estuary*

la fodera – *fodder*

il fonte battesimale – *baptismal font*

le forbici – *scissors*

la forcella – *fork*

il forfait chilometrico – *unlimited mileage*

la forfora – *dandruff*

il formaggio – *cheese*

il fornaio – *baker*

il fornello – *cooker*

la fortezza – *fortress*

il foulard – *winter scarf*

le fragole – *strawberries*

un frammento di pietra – *rough stone*

il frassino – *ash tree*

le freccie – *turn signal*

freddo – *cold (temp.)*

il freno a contrepedale – *pedal brake*

il freno a mano – *hand brake*

il freno sul cerchione – *calliper brake*

fresco – *fresh*

la frutta – *fruit*

i frutti di mare – *seafood*

il fruttivendolo – *fruit stand*

fumatori – *smoking*

il fusibile (valvola) – *fuse*

G

il gabbiano – *seagull*

il gabinetto – *toilet, WC*

la galeria – *gallery*

la galleria – *circle (theatre)*

il gasolio – *diesel*

gennaio – *January*

ghiaccio – *ice (on roads)*

la ghiaia – *gravel*

la giacca – *(dress) jacket*

giallo – *yellow*

il gardino – *garden*

il gardino all'inglese – *English garden*

il ginecologo – *gynecologist*

il ginocchio – *knee*

il gioco de birilli – *skittles, nine-pin bowling*

la gioielleria – *jeweller*

il giornalaio – *newsstand, news agent*

il giornale – *newspaper*

giovedì – *Thursday*

il giramento i stomaco – *nausea*

guigno – *June*

le gocce – *drops*

la gola – *neck*

il golf – *golf course*

il gomito – *elbow, angleiron, crowbar*

la gomma – *tire, rubber*

la gonna – *skirt*

il gotico – *Gothic*

il grammo – *gramme*

il grande magazzino – *department store*

il grande vagone – *open carriage*

il grano – *wheat*

il grappolo d'uva – *grape*

il grasso per la catena – *chain grease*

i greci – *Greeks*

grigio – *grey*

la griglia del radiatore – *cooler grille*

la grotta – *grotto, cave*

la grotta con stalattiti e stalagmiti – *cave with stalactites and stalagmites*

i guanti – *gloves*

il guardaroba – *cloakroom*

la guarnizione del freno – *brake lining*

guasto – *rotten, spoiled*

il guasto – *interference*

I

ieri – *yesterday*

l'imbarco – *departure gate*

l'immersione – *scuba diving*

le immondizie – *rubbish, garbage*

impanato – *breaded*

l'impermeabile – *rain cape, rain jacket, raincoat*

impianto di autolavaggio – *carwash*

in – *in*

l'incisione su rame – *engraving*

l'incrocio – *junction, intersection*

l'indictatore del livello della benzina – *fuel gauge*

l'infezione micosa – *fungal infection*

l'influenza – *flu*

le informazioni – *information*

l'ingessatura – *plastercast*

gli insetti – *insects*

l'insolazione – *sunstroke*

l'interruttore dell'accensione – *ignition switch*

l'intestino – *intestine*

l'intossicazione da alimenti – *food poisoning*

l'inverno – *winter*

il iogurt – *yogurt*

l'ippocastano – *horse chestnut*

l'ischialgia – *sciatica*

le iscrizioni rupestri – *cliff paintings*

l'itterizia – *jaundice*

J

i jeans – *jeans*

L

il laccio per scarpe – *shoelace*

il lago – *lake*

il lago artificiale – *reservoir*

Il laguna – *lagoon*

le lame – *razor blades*

la lampadina – *lightbulb*

la lampada di controllo – *warning light*

il lampeggiatore – *turn signal switch*

i lamponi – *raspberries*

la lana – *wool*

il latte – *milk*

la latteria – *dairy shop*

la lattina – *tin, can*

la lattuga – *head lettuce*

la lava – *lava*

il lavaggio – *main wash cycle*

la lavenderia – *laundrette, laundromat*

la lavandino – *lavatory, washroom*

lavare – *to wash*

la lavatrice – *washing machine*

il lavello – *sink*

lavori in corso – *construction work*
il legno – *wood*
le lenti a contatto – *contact lenses*
le lenticchie – *lentils*
lento – *slow*
la lenza – *fishing line*
il letto – *bed*
il letto per bambini – *child's bed*
la leva del cambio – *gear lever, stickshift*
libero – *free, unoccupied*
il liberty – *Art Nouveau*
la libreria – *bookstore, bookseller*
la libreria antiquaria – *second-hand book store*
il libro – *book*
la licenza di pesca – *fishing licence*
lilla – *purple*
la limetta da unghie – *nail file*
limitazione della velocità – *speed limit*
la limonata – *lemonade, soft drink*
il limone – *lemon*
la lingua – *tongue*
la lista – *menu*
il litro – *litre*
la lombaggine – *lumbago*
la lozione de barba – *aftershave*
il luccio – *pike*
la luce – *light*
la luce abbagliante – *high-beams*

la luce anteriore – *headlights*
la luce di posizione – *parking lights*
la luce posteriore – *tail lights*
la luce schermata – *low-beams*
la lucertola – *lizard*
luglio – *July*
la lumacha – *snail, escargo*
il lunedì – *Monday*
il luogo – *town, place*
il luogo di emissione – *place of issue*
il luogo di nascita – *place of birth*
il luogo di residenza – *place of residence*

M

ma – *but*
la macchia – *spot, stain*
la macchina – *car*
la macchina fotografica – *camera*
il macellaio – *butcher*
macinato – *ground*
il maestro/la maestra di sci – *ski instructor*
maggio – *May*
la maggiorana – *marjoram*
la maglia – *pullover, jumper, sweater*
la maglietta – *undershirt*
il maiale – *pig, pork*
la maionese – *mayonnaise*
il mais – *maize, corn*
il mal d'auto – *car (motion) sickness*

il mal di denti – *toothache*
il mal di gola – *sore throat*
il mal di testa – *headache*
il mal di ventre – *stomach ache*
la malaria – *malaria*
la malleolo – *ankle*
le mandorle – *almonds*
la manica – *sleeve*
il manicure – *manicure*
la maniglia della porta – *door handle, doorknob*
la mano (sing.)/le mani (pl.) – *hand(s)*
manubrio – *handlebars*
il manzo – *cow, beef*
il marciapiede – *train platform*
il mare – *sea, ocean*
la marmita catalitica – *catalytic converter*
il marmo – *marble*
marrone – *brown*
martedì – *Tuesday*
il martello – *hammer*
marzo – *March*
la maschera – *usher/usherette, facial*
il massaggio – *massage*
il massiccio – *mountain range (massif)*
il matroneo – *gallery, balcony*
la mattina – *morning*
di mattina – *during the morning*
il mattone – *brick*

la mazza de golf – *golf club*

il mazzo – *bunch*

il medico – *doctor, physician*

il medioevo – *Middle Ages*

il Mediterraneo – *Mediterranean*

la medusa – *jellyfish*

la mela – *apple*

la melanzana – *aubergine, eggplant*

il melone – *(honeydew) melon*

la menta – *mint*

il mercato – *market*

mercoledì – *Wednesday*

il merluzzo – *sea pike*

il merluzzo comune – *cod*

le mestruazioni – *menstruation*

il metro – *metre stick, metre*

il mezzo chilo – *pound (metric), 500 g*

(a) mezzogiorno – *(during) midday, noon*

il minigolf – *crazy golf, miniature golf*

il misuratore della pressione dell'aria – *air pressure gauge*

i mobili – *furniture*

il modulo – *form*

il modulo per una cura medica internazionale – *international health insurance form*

le montagne – *mountain range*

il monte – *mountain*

il morbillo – *measles*

il mosaico – *mosaic*

la moschea – *mosque*

la mostra – *exhibition*

la motocicletta – *motorcycle*

il motorino – *motor scooter*

il motorismo – *motor sport*

la mountainbike – *mountain bike*

il mozzo (della ruota) – *hub*

il municipio – *city hall*

il muro – *wall*

il museo – *museum*

le mutande – *underpants*

N

il naso – *nose*

il nastro adesivo – *adhesive tape*

Natale – *Christmas*

la navata – *nave*

la navata laterale – *side aisles*

navigare a vela – *sailing*

la nazionalitá – *nationality*

negozio di articoli elettrici – *electrical goods shop*

il negozio di articoli fotografici – *camera shop*

il negozoi di banchieria – *linens shop*

il negozio di calzature – *shoe shop*

il negozio di ferramenta – *ironmonger, hardware store*

il negozio di gioccattoli – *toy store*

il negozio di mobili – *furniture store*

il negozio di specialità gastronomiche – *delicatessen, gourmet food store*

il negozio di vini – *wine shop*

nero – *black*

i nervi – *nerves*

no – *no*

le nocciole – *hazelnuts*

le noccioline americane – *peanuts*

la noce – *walnut*

la noce del Pará – *Brazil nut*

la noce di coco – *coconut*

la noce moscata – *nutmeg*

le noci – *nuts*

il nome – *name*

il nome da nubile – *maiden name*

la notte – *night*

di notte – *at night*

novembre – *November*

il numero del volo – *flight number*

il numero dell'abbonato – *telephone number*

il numero della carrozza – *carriage number, wagon number (train)*

il nuoto – *swimming*

O

o – *or*
l'oca – *goose*
gli occhiali – *spectacles, glasses*
gli occhiali ba sole – *sunglasses*
l'occhiello – *buttonhole*
l'occhio – *eye*
occupato – *occupied, busy, engaged*
l'oculista – *eye doctor*
oggi – *today*
l'Ognissanti – *All Saints' Day*
l'olio – *oil*
l'olio per freni – *brake fluid*
l'olio per le macchine per cucire – *sewing machine oil*
l'olio solare – *suntan oil*
le olive – *olives*
l'olmo – *elm tree*
l'ombrello – *umbrella*
l'ontano – *alder*
l'ora d'arrivo – *arrival time*
l'ora di partenza – *departure time*
l'orario – *schedule, timetable*
l'orrechio – *ear*
l'origano – *oregano*
l'orlo – *seam*
l'orlogiaio – *watchmaker*
l'orologio – *watch*
l'orto botanico – *botanical garden*
l'ortopedico – *othopaedic surgeon*
l'ospedale – *hospital*

l'osservatorio – *observatory*
l'osso (sing.)/le ossa (pl.) – *bone(s)*
l'otite media – *middle ear infection*
l'otorinolaringoiatra – *ear, nose and throat specialist*
l'ottico – *optician*
ottobre – *October*
l'ovatta – *cotton wool*

P

il pacco – *package*
pacchetto – *packet*
il paesaggio – *landscape*
il palco – *box (theatre)*
la palla a mano – *handball*
la pallacanestro – *basketball*
la pallavolo – *volleyball*
il palo da tenda – *tent pole*
la palpebra – *eyelid*
il panciotto, il gil – *vest*
il pane – *bread*
i panini – *bread roll, hard roll*
la panna da cucina – *sour cream*
la panne dolce – *whipping cream*
il pannello portastrumenti – *dashboard*
i pannolini – *nappies, diapers*
il panorama – *panorama*
i pantaloncini corti – *shorts*

i pantaloni – *trousers, slacks*
il parabrezza – *windscreen, windshield*
il paraccadutismo – *parachuting*
il parafango – *wing, fender (car), mudguard (bicycle)*
parapendio – *paragliding*
il paraurti – *bumper*
parchimetro – *parking meter*
il parco di protezione degli uccelli – *bird sanctuary*
il parco nazionale – *national park, nature reserve??*
la parotite – *mumps*
la parrucca – *wig*
il parruchiere – *hairdresser*
la partenza – *departure*
Pasqua – *Easter*
passaggio a livello – *level crossing*
le paste – *pasta, noodles*
la pasticceria – *confectonery, pastry shop*
le patate – *potatoes*
la patente – *driving licence*
il pattinaggio su ghiaccio – *ice skating*
il pattino del freno – *brake shoe*
pedaggio (autostradale) – *(motorway/highway) toll*
il pedale – *pedal*

il pedale del freno – *brake pedal*

il pedale dell'acceleratore – *accellorator pedal*

il pediatra – *paediatrician*

il pedicure – *pedicure*

la pelle – *skin, leather*

la pelletteria – *leather goods*

il pennello – *brush*

il pennello da barba – *shaving brush*

Pentecoste – *Pentecost*

il pepe – *pepper*

peproncini – *hot peppers*

il peperone – *green pepper, sweet pepper, bell pepper*

per favore – *please*

la pera – *pear*

perchè – *because*

il pericolo – *danger*

il periodico – *magazine*

la permanente – *perm(anent)*

però – *but, however*

la pesca – *peach*

la pesca d'alto mare – *deep-sea fishing*

pescare con l'amo – *fishing*

il pesce – *fish*

la pescheria – *fish store*

il petrolio – *paraffin, kerosine*

il pettine – *comb*

il petto – *breast, chest*

i piatti – *crockery, dishes*

il piatto – *plate*

la piazza – *square, plaza*

il picchetto – *tent peg*

il piede – *foot*

il piedistallo – *pedestal*

la pietra – *stone*

pietrisco – *loose chippings, loose gravel*

il piggione – *pigeon*

il pigiama – *pyjama*

la pila – *battery (small)*

il pilastro – *pillar*

il pino – *pine*

il pino silvestre – *Scotch pine*

le pinze per tubi – *pipe wrench*

il piombo – *lead*

il pioppo – *poplar*

i piselli – *peas*

la pista – *track*

la pista ciclabile – *bike path, trail*

la pista di fondo – *cross-country trail*

i pistacchi – *pistachios*

il platano – *plane tree*

il pneumatico – *tire*

il pneumatico sgonfio – *flat tire*

il poggiatesta – *headrest*

il pollice – *thumb*

il polio – *chicken*

il polmone – *lung*

il polpaccio – *calf (leg)*

la pomata – *ointment*

di pomeriggio – *in the afternoon*

il pomeriggio – *afternoon*

i pomodori – *tomatoes*

la pompa – *pump*

la pompa dell'olio – *oil pump*

il pompelmo – *grapefruit*

il ponte – *bridge*

il pony – *fringe, bangs*

la porcellana – *porcelain*

il porro – *leeks*

il portabagagli – *carrier (bicycle), boot, trunk (car)*

il portale – *portal*

il portone – *gate*

le posate – *cutlery, silverware*

il posteggio – *bicycle stand*

il posto – *seat*

un posto accanto al finestrino – *window seat*

il posto per cucinare – *cooking area*

il pranzo – *lunch*

praticare il surfing – *surfing*

il prato – *meadow*

il precipizio – *canyon, ravine*

il prefisso nazionale – *country code*

il prefisso telefonico – *trunk code, area code*

prego – *please, here you are*

il prelavaggio – *pre-wash cycle*

il prenome – *given name, first name*

la prenotazione – *reservation*

la prescrizione – *prescription*

i preservativi – *condoms*

la pressione delle gomme – *tire pressure*

il prezzemolo – *parsley*

il prezzo – *price*

la prima classe – *first class*

la prima colazione – *breakfast*

la primavera – *spring (season)*

le prime file della platea – *stalls (theatre)*

il primo /secondo piatto – *(first/second) main course*

principianti/non principianti – *beginner/advanced*

la professione – *occupation*

il programma – *programme*

prossimo(a) – *next*

la prugna – *plum*

pulire a secco – *to clean*

il pullover – *sweater, jumper*

il pullover senza maniche – *slipover, sleveless sweater*

Q

il quadrato – *crossroads, junction*

il quadro – *painting*

la quaglia – *quail*

la qualcosa – *snack*

quando – *when?*

quasi – *almost*

la querica – *oak*

R

la racchetta (da tennis) – *tennis racket*

il radiatore – *radiator*

la radio – *radio*

il rafano – *radish*

il raffreddore – *cold (illness)*

i raggi – *spokes*

rallentare – *drive slowly*

la rana – *frog*

il rasolo – *electric shaver*

il ravanello – *radish (small)*

la recezione – *reception*

il recipiente – *vessel*

la registrazione – *booking*

il reggiseno – *bra*

il rene – *kidney*

la rete portabagagli – *luggage rack*

il retrovisore – *rearview mirror*

i ribes – *currants*

il riccio di mare – *sea urchin*

la ricevuta – *receipt*

la ricotta – *ricotta cheese*

il rifletorre – *reflector*

il rigattiere – *secondhand shop*

il rimedio contro la tosse – *cough remedy*

rimettere l'acqua nel radiatore – *refill the coolant*

rimorchio – *trailer*

il rinascimento – *Renaissance*

il riscaldamento – *heater, heating*

il riso – *rice*

il ristorante della stazione – *station restaurant*

il ritardo – *delay*

il rivetto – *rivet*

la rivista – *magazine*

la roccia – *rock*

i romani – *Romans*

il romanico – *Romanesque*

il romanticismo – *Romantic (period)*

il ronzio auricolare – *buzzing in the ears*

rosa – *pink*

la rosetta – *washer*

il rosmarino – *rosemary*

la rosolia – *rubella, German measles*

il rospo – *toad*

rosso – *red*

la rotonda – *roundabout, traffic circle*

la roulotte – *caravan, camper*

la rovina – *ruin(s)*

la ruota – *wheel*

la ruota anteriore – *front wheel*

la ruota di scorta – *spare wheel*

la ruota posteriore – *rear wheel*

il ruscello – *stream, brook*

S

sabato – *Saturday*

la sabbia – *sand*

la sabbia mobile – *quicksand*
il sacchetto – *bag*
il sacchetto delle immondizie – *rubbish bag, garbage bag*
la sala d'attesa – *waiting hall*
il sale – *salt*
il salice – *willow*
il salice piangente – *weeping willow*
le salsiccette – *sausages*
la salsiccia – *sausage*
la salvia – *sage*
i sandali – *sandals*
il sapone – *soap*
il sapone de barba – *shaving soap*
il sarcofago – *sarcophagus*
la sartoria – *tailor*
la sauna – *sauna*
le scale – *stairs*
le scale mobili – *escalator*
lo scalpello – *chisel*
lo scappamento – *exhaust pipe*
lo scarico – *drain*
le scarpe – *shoes*
le scarpe de bagno – *bathing shoes*
lo scatto – *telephone fee unit*
gli scavi – *excavations*
la schiena – *back*
gli sci – *skis*
lo sci acquatico – *water skiing*
lo sci di fondo – *cross-country skiing*

lo sci in discesa – *downhill skiing*
lo sciare – *skiing*
la sciarpa da collo – *neck scarf*
la sciolina – *ski wax*
lo sciroppo contro la tosse – *cough syrup*
lo scompartimento – *train compartment*
lo scorpione – *scorpion*
la scottatura – *burn*
la scottatura solare – *sunburn*
la scultura – *sculpture*
le sculture – *sculptures*
la scuola – *school*
scuro – *brown (skin, hair)*
scuro – *dark*
se – *if*
secco – *dried*
il secolo – *century*
la seconda classe – *second class*
il sedano – *cellery*
il sedile a fianco del conduttore – *passenger seat*
il sedile del conducente – *driver's seat*
il sedile per bambini – *child's seat*
la sega – *saw*
la segala – *rye*
la seggiovia – *chairlift*
il segnale d'allarme – *emergency brake*
self-service – *self-service*
la sella – *bicycle seat*
selvaggina vagante – *game crossing*

il semaforo – *traffic light*
sempre diritto – *straight on, straight ahead*
il senape – *mustard*
senso unico – *one-way street*
senza – *without*
senza piombo – *unleaded, lead-free*
la sera – *evening*
di sera – *during the evening*
il serbatoio – *tank*
il serpente – *snake*
la serratura della porta – *door lock*
il servizio – *service*
settembre – *September*
la settimana – *week*
la shampoo – *shampoo*
gli shorts – *shorts*
si – *yes*
le sigarette – *cigarettes*
il sigaretto – *cigarillo*
il sigaro – *cigar*
la sinagoga – *synagogue*
a sinistra – *to the left*
lo ski-lift – *ski lift*
la slitta – *sledding*
la slogatura – *sprain*
la soluzione per la conservazione – *soaking solution (contact lenses)*
la soluzione sterilizzante – *cleaning solution (contact lenses)*
il sonnifero – *sleeping pills*
sopra – *above*

le sopracciglie – *eye-brows*

la sorgente – *spring (water)*

sotto – *under*

la spalliera – *seatback*

la spatola – *stripping knife*

la spazzola per i capelli – *hairbrush*

la spazzola per le stoviglie – *dish brush*

lo spazzolino da denti – *toothbrush*

lo specchietto esterno – *outside mirror*

lo specchio – *mirror*

la spia (luminosa) – *hazard warning light*

la spiaggia – *beach*

la spilla di sicurezza – *safety pin*

lo spinacio – *spinach*

lo spirito – *spirits, rubbing alcohol*

lo sport della canoa – *canoeing*

lo sportello accettazione bagagli – *luggage counter*

lo sportello d'auto – *car door*

lo spuntone – *promontory*

lo stagno – *pond*

stamattina – *this morning*

la stampa – *print*

stasera – *this evening*

la statua – *statue*

la stazione – *train station*

lo stile floreale – *Art Nouveau*

lo stinco – *shin*

lo stiramento del tendine – *pulled tendon*

stirare – *to iron*

gli stivali – *boots*

gli stivali di gomma – *wellingtons, galoshes*

la stoffa – *fabric, material*

lo stomaco – *stomach*

lo straccio per lavare i piatti – *dish cloth*

la strada – *road, street*

la strada di raccordo – *bypass*

strada sdrucciolevole – *slippery road*

lo strappo – *torn ligament*

lo strappo muscolare – *torn muscle*

lo stretto – *strait*

strettoia – *road narrows*

a strisce – *striped*

lo strofinaccio per lavarsi – *washcloth, face flannel*

lo studio medico – *treatment room*

stufato – *steamed*

su – *on*

il succo di frutta – *juice*

il sund – *sound (geol.)*

T

il T-shirt – *T-shirt*

la tabaccheria – *tobacconist*

il tabacco – *tobacco*

la tacchina – *turkey*

il tachimetro – *speedometer*

tagliato a fette – *sliced*

il taglio a gradini – *layered cut*

il tailleur – *ladies' suit*

il tampone – *tampon*

la tanica – *canister*

il tappo del serbatoio – *fuel cap*

il tappo della benzina – *fuel filler neck*

il tascapane per bicicletta – *pannier bag*

la tascha – *bag*

la tassa – *fees*

il té – *tea*

il teatro – *theatre*

il telaio – *frame*

la telefonata R – *reversed charges, collect call*

il telefono – *telephone*

il televisore – *television*

il tempio – *temple*

le tenaglie – *pliers*

la tenda – *tent*

il tennis – *tennis*

il tennis da tavolo – *table tennis, ping-pong*

la tenuta da sci – *ski suit*

il tergicristallo – *windscreen wipers, windshield wipers*

il termometro – *thermometer*

la tessera annua – *annual pass*

la tessera di campeggio – *camping permit*

la tessera di pesca – *fishing permit*

il tessuto – *fabric, material*
la testa – *head*
il tetano – *tetanus*
il tetto – *roof*
il timo – *thyme*
tinchè – *until*
tingere i capelli – *hair tinting*
la tintura – *tincture*
la tonsillite – *tonsilitis*
la torcia – *pocket lamp, flashlight*
il torre – *tower*
la tosse – *coughing*
il toupet – *toupet*
tra – *between*
il traffico in senso contrario – *oncoming traffic*
il traliccio – *half-timber*
il trapano (meccanico) – *(electric) drill*
la trasmissione su tutte le ruote – *four-wheel drive*
la traspirazione – *sweating*
il trattamento per i capelli – *hair treatment*
la trazione anteriore – *front-wheel drive*
la trazione posteriore – *rear-wheel drive*
il treno diretto – *direct train*
il treno espresso – *express train*
il treno locale – *local train*
il treno navetta – *car sleeper train*
la trota – *trout*

truccare – *make-up*
il tubo – *tube, hose*
il tubo di respirazione – *snorkel*

U

gli uccelli – *birds*
l'uccello rapace – *bird of prey*
l'ufficio guasti – *telephone service department*
umido – *wet*
l'unghia – *fingernail*
l'uovo (sing.) le uova (plural) – *egg(s)*
l'uscita – *exit*
l'utilitaria – *compact car*
l'uva – *grape*
l'uva secca – *raisin*

V

la vacca – *cow*
la vaccinazione – *vaccination*
il vagone letto – *sleeper car*
il vagone-ristorante – *restaurant car*
la valle – *valley*
la valvola – *valve*
la varicella – *chickenpox*
il veicolo per marcia fuori strada – *off-road vehicle*
veloce – *fast*
venerdì – *Friday*
il venerdì santo – *Good Friday*
la ventilazzione – *fan*
il ventre – *abdomen*
verde – *green*
le verdure – *vegetables*

il verme da pesca – *bait*
la vescica – *bladder*
il vestito – *dress*
il vetro – *glass*
la via – *street*
la viale alberato – *boulevard*
vicino – *near*
vietato – *prohibited*
vietato fumare – *non-smoking*
vietato sorpassare – *do not overtake, do not pass*
i vigneti – *vineyards*
la villa (signorile) – *manorhouse*
il vincolo – *alleyway*
il vino – *wine*
la vipera – *viper*
la vite – *screw*
il vitello – *veal*
il volante – *steering wheel*
il volare a vela – *gliding*
il volo di andata – *one-way flight*
il volo di coincidenza – *connecting flight*
il volo di ritorno – *return flight*
il vomito – *vomiting*
il vulcano – *volcano*

Z

lo zafferano – *saffron*
la zanzara – *mosquito, gnat*
lo zoo – *zoo*
la zucca – *squash*
lo zucchero – *sugar*
le zucchine – *zucchini*
la zuppa – *soup*